SEXUAL OFFENCES ACT 2003

EXPLANATORY NOTES

INTRODUCTION

1. These explanatory notes relate to the Sexual Offences Act 2003 which received Royal Assent on 20 November 2003. They have been prepared by the Home Office in order to assist the reader in understanding the Act. They do not form part of the Act and have not been endorsed by Parliament.

2. The notes need to be read in conjunction with the act. they are not, and are not meant to be, a comprehensive description of the act. so where a section or part of a section does not seem to require any explanation or comment, none is given.

3. Part 1 of the Act extends only to England and Wales, with the exception of sections 15-24, 46-54, 57-60, 66 to 72, 78 and 79 which extend to Northern Ireland. Part 2 of the Act extends to England, Wales, Northern Ireland and, save for sections 93 and 123-129, Scotland.

BACKGROUND

4. The Government published the White Paper *Protecting the Public: strengthening protection against sex offenders and reforming the law on sexual offences* (Cm 5668) in November 2002. It is available on the Home Office website at www.sexualoffencesbill.homeoffice.gov.uk. The White Paper set out the Government's intentions for reforming the law on sexual offences and for strengthening measures to protect the public from sexual offending. The Government's proposals were based on the recommendations made by two review teams and subsequent public consultation. The recommendations made by the review teams were published in two documents: *Review of Part 1 of the Sex Offenders Act 1997* (2001) and *Setting the Boundaries* (2000).

SUMMARY

5. The Act is in three Parts:

6. Part 1 makes new provision about sexual offences. It covers the non-consensual offences of rape, assault by penetration, sexual assault and causing a person to engage in sexual activity without consent. It defines "consent" and "sexual" and sets out evidential and conclusive presumptions about consent. It covers child sex offences and offences involving an abuse of a position of trust towards a child. Familial child sex offences and offences involving adult relatives are provided for, as are offences designed to give protection to persons with a mental disorder. The age of a "child" in the Protection of Children Act 1978 has been amended to 18, and defences are provided for in limited cases where the child is 16 or over and the defendant is the child's partner. A limited defence is also introduced to the offence of "making" an indecent photograph or pseudo-photograph of a child where the purpose of the "making" is to combat crime. This Part also covers offences relating to prostitution, child pornography, and trafficking. It provides for preparatory offences, such as administering a substance with intent to commit a sexual offence, and a number of

miscellaneous offences, such as voyeurism and intercourse with an animal. Section 72 provides that there is extra-territorial jurisdiction for many acts which, if committed in England and Wales or Northern Ireland, would amount to offences under Part 1 committed against a child under 16 or (in the case of Northern Ireland) under 17. The Part extends to England and Wales and some provisions also extend to Northern Ireland.

7.   Part 2 contains measures for protecting the public from sexual harm. Part 1 of the Sex Offenders Act 1997 has been re-enacted with a number of amendments. A notification order enabling the notification requirements to be applied to offenders with convictions abroad has been created. Sex offender orders (s.2 of Crime and Disorder Act 1998) and restraining orders (s.5 of Sex Offenders Act 1997) have been combined into a new civil preventative order – a sexual offences prevention order. Risk of sexual harm orders, specifically designed to protect children from sexual harm, have been created, as have foreign travel orders, which can be used to prevent an offender with a conviction for a sex offence against a child from travelling to countries where he is at risk of abusing children. Part 2 extends to England and Wales and Northern Ireland, and, save for Schedule 4 and the risk of sexual harm orders, to Scotland.

8.   Part 3 contains general provisions relating to the Act, including minor and consequential amendments and commencement provisions.

TERRITORIAL APPLICATION: WALES

9.   The Act does not affect the powers of the National Assembly for Wales.

COMMENTARY ON SECTIONS

Part 1: Sexual Offences

Section 1: Rape

10. Section 1 makes it an offence for a person (A) intentionally to penetrate with his penis the vagina, anus or mouth of another person (B) without that person's consent if A does not reasonably believe that B consents. *Subsection (2)* provides that whether a belief in consent is reasonable is to be determined having regard to all the circumstances, including any steps A has taken to ascertain whether B consents. This and the offence in section 5 are the only offences that can only be committed by a male, because they relate to penile penetration. *Subsection (3)* provides that sections 75 and 76 apply to this offence. Sections 75 and 76 deal with evidential and conclusive presumptions about consent.

Section 2: Assault by penetration

11. Section 2 covers the situation where a person (A) intentionally penetrates the vagina or anus of another person (B). The offence is committed where the penetration is by a part of A's body (for example, a finger) or anything else, (for example, a bottle); where the penetration is sexual (as defined in section 78), so that it excludes, for example, intimate searches and medical procedures; where B does not consent to the penetration; and where A does not reasonably believe that B consents. What is said in the note to section 1 about whether a belief in consent is reasonable also applies here. This and all subsequent offences in the Bill save the offence at section 5 can be committed by a male or female, against a male or female. *Subsection (3)* provides that sections 75 and 76 apply to this offence. Sections 75 and 76 deal with evidential and conclusive presumptions about consent.

Section 3: Sexual assault

12. Section 3 makes it an offence for a person (A) intentionally to touch sexually another person (B) without that person's consent, if he does not reasonably believe that B consents. What is said in the note to section 1 about whether a belief in consent is reasonable also applies here. The meaning of "touching" is explained at section 79(8); "sexual" is defined at section 78. The effect of these sections is that the offence covers a wide range of behaviour including, for example, rubbing up against someone's private parts through the person's clothes for sexual gratification. *Subsection (3)* provides that sections 75 and 76 apply to this offence. Sections 75 and 76 deal with evidential and conclusive presumptions about consent.

Section 4: Causing a person to engage in sexual activity without consent

13. Section 4 makes it an offence for a person (A) intentionally to cause another person (B) to engage in sexual activity (as defined in section 78) without that person's consent, if he does not reasonably believe that B consents. What is said in the note to section 1 about whether a belief in consent is reasonable also applies here. A may cause B to engage in sexual activity with A (for example, a woman who compels a man to penetrate her); on B himself (for example, where one person forces someone else to masturbate himself); or with another person (for example, where one person makes someone else masturbate a third person). *Subsection (3)* provides that sections 75 and 76 apply to this offence. Sections 75 and 76 deal with evidential and conclusive presumptions about consent.

Section 5: Rape of a child under 13

14. Section 5 makes it an offence for a person intentionally to penetrate with his penis the vagina, anus or mouth of a child under the age of 13. Whether or not the child consented to this act is irrelevant.

Section 6: Assault of a child under 13 by penetration

15. Section 6 makes it an offence for a person intentionally to penetrate sexually the vagina or anus of a child under the age of 13 with a part of his body, such as a finger, or with anything else, such as bottle or other object. The penetration must be sexual, as defined in section 78. Whether or not the child consented to the act is irrelevant.

Section 7: Sexual assault of a child under 13

16. Section 7 makes it an offence for a person to touch sexually a child under the age of 13. The meanings of "touching" and "sexual" are the same as for section 3. Whether or not the child consented to the act is irrelevant.

Section 8: Causing or inciting a child under 13 to engage in sexual activity

17. Section 8 makes it an offence for a person intentionally to cause or incite a child under the age of 13 to engage in sexual activity. In relation to caused sexual activity, the offence covers the same situations as does the offence under section 4 except that, for this offence, whether or not the child consented to engaging in the sexual activity is irrelevant. This section also covers the situation where incitement takes place but the sexual activity itself does not. For example, a person may incite a child to engage in sexual activity with him (for example, where a person incites the child to masturbate him), or on the child himself (for example, where a person incites the child to strip) or with a third person (for example, where someone incites the child to have sexual intercourse with his friend).

Section 9: Sexual activity with a child

18.   Section 9 makes it an offence for a person (A) aged 18 or over to intentionally engage in sexual touching of a child under 16. Where the child is aged 13 or over but under 16, the prosecution must prove that A did not reasonably believe that he was 16 or over. "Touching" is explained at section 79(8) and covers all forms of physical contact including penetration; "sexual" is defined at section 78. Whether or not the child consented to the activity is irrelevant.

Section 10: Causing or inciting a child to engage in sexual activity

19.   Section 10 makes it an offence for a person (A) aged 18 or over, intentionally to cause or incite a child aged under 16 to engage in sexual activity (as defined at section 78). Where the child is aged 13 or over, but under 16, the prosecution must prove that A did not reasonably believe that he was 16 or over. The sexual activity which is caused or incited may be activity with A (for example, where A causes or incites the child to have sexual intercourse with him), on the child himself (for example, where A causes or incites the child to strip for A's sexual gratification) or with a third person (for example, where A causes or incites the child to have sexual intercourse with A's friend). The incitement constitutes an offence whether or not the activity incited actually takes place. Whether or not the child consented to the activity caused or incited, or to the incitement, is irrelevant.

Section 11: Engaging in sexual activity in the presence of a child

20. Section 11 makes it an offence for a person (A) aged 18 or over intentionally to engage in sexual activity (as defined in section 78), in order to gain sexual gratification, when a child aged under 16 is present or in a place from which A can be observed. Where the child is aged 13 or over but under 16, the prosecution must prove that A did not reasonably believe that he was 16 or over. The offence is committed if A knows or believes that the child is aware that he is engaging in the activity or intends that the child should be aware of this. This offence would cover, for example, A masturbating himself in front of a child, or A masturbating himself in the presence of the child to whom he is describing what he is doing, perhaps because the child is covering his face. It would also cover the situation where A performs a sexual act in a place where he knows that he can be seen by a child, for example via a webcam.

Section 12: Causing a child to watch a sexual act

21. Section 12 makes it an offence for a person (A) intentionally to cause a child aged under 16, for the purpose of the sexual gratification of A, to watch a third person engaging in sexual activity or to look at an image of a person engaging in sexual activity. Where the child is aged 13 or over but under 16, the prosecution must prove that A did not reasonably believe that he was 16 or over. The definition of sexual activity is at section 78. A person who, for his own sexual gratification, forces a child to watch two people have sex, or who forces a child to watch a pornographic film, would commit this offence.

Section 13: Child sex offences committed by children or young persons

22. Section 13 makes it an offence for a person aged under 18 to do anything that would be an offence under any of sections 9 to 12 if he were aged 18 or over. The purpose of this section is to provide a lower penalty where the offender is aged under 18. In practice (although there is no provision about this in the Act) decisions on whether persons under 18

should be charged with child sex offences will be made by Crown Prosecutors in accordance with the principles set out in the Code for Crown Prosecutors. In deciding whether it is in the public interest to prosecute these offences, where there is enough evidence to provide a realistic prospect of conviction, prosecutors may take into consideration factors such as the ages of the parties; the emotional maturity of the parties; whether they entered into a sexual relationship willingly; any coercion or corruption by a person; and the relationship between the parties and whether there was any existence of a duty of care or breach of trust.

Section 14: Arranging or facilitating commission of a child sex offence

23. Section 14 makes it an offence for a person (A) intentionally to arrange or facilitate any action which he intends to do, intends another person to do or believes that another person will do, in any part of the world, which will involve an offence being committed against a child under any of sections 9 to 13.

24. An example of the first two limbs of the offence is where A approaches an agency requesting the agency to procure a child for the purpose of sexual activity either with himself or with a friend. The offence is committed whether or not the sex takes place. An example of the third limb of the offence is where A intentionally drives another person (X) to meet a child with whom he knows X is going to have sexual activity. A may not intend X to have child sexual activity, but he believes that X will do so if he meets that child.

25. *Subsection (2)* provides an exception for anyone whose actions are intended to protect the child. *Subsection (3)* defines the concept of acting for the protection of a child as acting to protect a child from pregnancy or sexually transmitted infection, to protect the physical safety of a child or to promote the emotional wellbeing of a child by the giving of advice. The exception only applies if the person is not causing or encouraging an activity that would constitute an offence under sections 9 to 13 and if he is not acting for the purpose of obtaining sexual gratification. An example would be where a health worker believes that a person is having sex with a child under 16. He advises that it is unlawful to have sex with children under 16 but supplies him with condoms because he believes that the person will otherwise have sex with the child without using any protection.

Section 15: Meeting a child following sexual grooming etc.

26. Section 15 makes it an offence for a person (A) aged 18 or over to meet intentionally, or to travel with the intention of meeting, a child aged under 16 in any part of the world, if he has met or communicated with that child on at least two earlier occasions, and intends to commit a "relevant offence" against that child either at the time of the meeting or on a subsequent occasion. An offence is not committed if A reasonably believes the child to be 16 or over.

27. The section is intended to cover situations where an adult (A) establishes contact with a child through, for example, meetings, telephone conversations or communications on the Internet, and gains the child's trust and confidence so that he can arrange to meet the child for the purpose of committing a "relevant offence" against the child. The course of conduct prior to the meeting that triggers the offence may have an explicitly sexual content, such as A entering into conversations with the child about the sexual acts he wants to engage her in when they meet, or sending images of adult pornography. However, the prior meetings or communication need not have an explicitly sexual content and could for example simply be A giving the child swimming lessons or meeting her incidentally through a friend.

28. The offence will be complete either when, following the earlier communications, A meets the child or travels to meet the child with the intent to commit a relevant offence against the child. The intended offence does not have to take place.

29. The evidence of A's intent to commit an offence may be drawn from the communications between A and the child before the meeting or may be drawn from other circumstances, for example if A travels to the meeting with ropes, condoms and lubricants.

30. *Subsection (2)(a)* provides that A's previous meetings or communications with the child can have taken place in or across any part of the world. This would cover for example A emailing the child from abroad, A and the child speaking on the telephone abroad, or A meeting the child abroad. The travel to the meeting itself must at least partly take place in England or Wales or Northern Ireland.

Section 16: Abuse of position of trust: sexual activity with a child

Section 17: Abuse of position of trust: causing or inciting a child to engage in sexual activity

Section 18: Abuse of position of trust: sexual activity in the presence of a child

Section 19: Abuse of position of trust: causing a child to watch a sexual act

31. These sections re-enact and amend the offence of abuse of position of trust under sections 3 and 4 of the Sexual Offences (Amendment) Act 2000. The sections each provide that it is an offence for a person (A) aged 18 or over intentionally to behave in certain sexual ways in relation to a child aged under 18, where A is in a position of trust (as defined in section 21) in respect of the child. The prohibited behaviour in each of the sections is identical to that prohibited by the child sex offences in sections 9, 10, 11 and 12 respectively, except that for the abuse of position of trust offences, the child may be 16 or 17.

32. Except where the child is under 13, one of the requirements of the offence is that A does not reasonably believe that the child is 18 or over, and A is subject to an evidential burden in relation to this aspect of the offence (*subsection (3)* of each section). An evidential burden means that, unless A shows from the evidence that there is an arguable case as to whether he reasonably believed the child to be 18 or over, it is presumed that he did not reasonably believe this. Where the child is under 13, the offence is committed regardless of any belief A might have in relation to the child's age.

33. The effect of *subsection (1)(d)* (or in the case of section 18, *subsection (1)(e)*) is that, where A is in a position of trust by virtue of one of the first four categories of position of trust set out at section 21, the prosecution must prove, in addition to the other requirements, that he knew or could reasonably have been expected to know of the facts placing him in a position of trust with the child. *Subsection (4)* of each section puts an evidential burden on A in this respect. This means that, unless A shows from the evidence that there is an arguable case as to whether or not he knew or could reasonably have been expected to know of the facts giving rise to the position of trust, it is presumed that he did know or could reasonably have been expected to know them. The first four categories of position of trust all concern situations where A looks after persons under 18 at an institution and the child is at that institution. Subsection (4) is designed to cover cases where, for example, the institution where A works is very large or has a number of different sites, and A may not therefore know that the child is at the institution.

Section 20: Abuse of position of trust: acts done in Scotland

34. Section 20 provides that any act that would, if done in England, Wales or Northern Ireland, constitute an offence under sections 16 to 19 of this Act, also constitutes an offence under those sections if carried out in Scotland.

Section 21: Positions of trust

Section 22: Positions of trust: interpretation

35. Section 21 defines "position of trust" for the purposes of the offences in sections 16, 17, 18 and 19. *Subsection (1)(b)* of section 21 also provides a power for the Secretary of State to specify further conditions that will constitute a position of trust. The power is subject to the affirmative parliamentary procedure (section 137(2)).

36. The conditions in *subsections (2)* to *(5)* use the term "looks after". This term is defined, in broad terms, at *subsection (2)* of section 22.

37. *Subsection (2)* applies where the child is detained following conviction for a criminal offence, for example in a secure training centre or a young offenders institution.

38. *Subsection (3)* applies to a wide range of settings in which young people are accommodated, including foster care; residential care (local authority, private or voluntary, including secure accommodation); and semi-independent accommodation.

39. *Subsection (4)* covers places where young people with medical conditions, physical or learning disabilities, mental illness or behavioural problems might be accommodated and includes NHS, private and voluntary accommodation.

40. *Subsection (5)* covers the situation where the child is receiving education in an educational institution. This concept is further explained at *subsection (4)* of section 22. The effect of that subsection is that where the child is registered at a college but receives education at another college with which the former has arrangements, A will still be in a position of trust in relation to the child if A works at the former college.

41. *Subsection (6)* covers children's guardians appointed under Northern Ireland legislation.

42. *Subsection (7)* includes persons who, in their capacity as, for example, Connexions Personal Advisers ("CPAs") look after children on an individual basis. The definition of looking after a child on an individual basis, for the purposes of this subsection, and *subsections (10) (11)* and *(13)* is at section 22(3). The reference at this definition to contact "by other means" (section 22(3)) is designed to include persons such as CPAs whose normal means of providing support to children is by telephone or via the Internet.

43. *Subsection (8)* covers those who have unsupervised contact with children in the context of their duties under section 20 or 21 of the Children Act 1989 and equivalent legislation in Northern Ireland. Such persons arrange accommodation for children who, for whatever reason, are not being looked after by those who have parental responsibility for them, and check that their welfare is being looked after once such accommodation has been found. They include local authority staff such as social workers and family centre staff who visit the accommodation in which a child has been placed in order to oversee the child's welfare.

44. *Subsection (9)* covers persons who have unsupervised contact with children by virtue of their appointment as children and family reporters under section 7 of the Children Act 1989

or under Article 4 of the Children (Northern Ireland) Order 1995. These persons present reports for the court relating to children's welfare.

45. *Subsection (10)* covers personal advisers who look after children on an individual basis (as defined at section 22(3)) having been appointed by a local authority under the Children Act 1989. Such personal advisers generally provide help and support to children aged 16-17 who have been in local authority care.

46. *Subsection (11)* covers persons who supervise children pursuant to a care order, supervision order or educational supervision order under various provisions in the Children Act 1989 or the Children (Northern Ireland) Order 1995 and, in that capacity, look after children on an individual basis (again, as defined at section 22(3)).

47. *Subsection (12)* covers a range of persons who, in the course of their duties, regularly have unsupervised contact with children. These are officers of the Children and Family Court Advisory and Support Service appointed to act as children's guardians under section 41(1) of the Children Act 1989; persons appointed as children's guardians in relation to adoption proceedings under Rules 6 and 18 of the Adoption Rules 1984; and persons appointed under Rule 9.5 of the Family Proceedings Rules 1991 to act as children's guardians ad litem in private law Children Act 1989 proceedings and cases determining wardship.

48. *Subsection (13)* includes adults who supervise children under bail supervision, a community sentence (for example a probation order, combination order, community service order, supervision order, attendance centre order) and children under conditions following release from detention resulting from a criminal conviction (e.g. those released on licence from a young offenders institution) This would include members of Youth Offending Teams provided they have sufficient contact and connection with the child or someone providing counselling or drug rehabilitation services to the child pursuant to the terms of a court order.

Section 23: Sections 16 to 19: marriage exception

49. Section 23 provides that A will not commit an offence under sections 16 to 19 if he can prove that, at the time of the sexual activity, B was aged 16 or over and he and B were lawfully married to each other.

Section 24: Sections 16 to 19: sexual relationships which pre-date position of trust

50. Section 24 provides A with a defence to abuse of position of trust offences if he can prove that his sexual relationship with B pre-dated his relationship of trust with B. So if A could prove that he and B had a sexual relationship before A went to work at the school at which B is a pupil, he would not commit an offence by continuing that sexual relationship. The effect of *subsection (2)* is to limit this to the situation where the sexual relationship that pre-dated the relationship of trust was lawful, so it would not cover for example a relationship with a child of under 16.

Section 25: Sexual activity with a child family member

51. Section 25 makes it an offence for a person (A) intentionally to touch a family member (as defined in sections 27) aged under 18, where the touching is sexual. The meaning of touching is explained at section 79(8). It covers all forms of physical contact including sexual intercourse. The definition of sexual is at section 78. Additional elements of the offence are that A must know, or be in a position where he could reasonably be expected to know, that

the child is his family member and that, except where the child is under 13, he does not reasonably believe that the child is 18 or over.

52. So if, for example, A has never met the child before, and so does not know, and could not reasonably be expected to know, that she is his sister, and reasonably believes she is over 18, he will not commit this offence by engaging in sexual activity with her, even though she is in fact his sister, and only 14.

53. In relation to both these last two elements of the offence A is under an evidential burden (*subsections (2) and (3)*). This means that unless A shows from the evidence that there is an arguable case about these issues, it is presumed that he did not reasonably believe the child to be 18 or over, and that he knew or could reasonably have been expected to know that the child was his family member. Whether or not the child consented to the touching is irrelevant.

Section 26: Inciting a child family member to engage in sexual activity

54. Section 26 makes it an offence for a person (A) intentionally to incite a child family member (defined in section 27) aged under 18 either to touch A or to allow himself to be touched by A, where the touching is sexual. The meaning of touching is at section 79(8). It covers all forms of physical contact including sexual intercourse. The definition of sexual is at section 78. An example of this offence would be where A encourages B to masturbate A or cajoles B into agreeing to have sex with him. The offence is committed whether or not the sexual touching takes place. So where in the above example A has encouraged B to masturbate him, but the masturbation does not take place because another person enters the room, the offence is nevertheless complete. The two additional elements of the offence (and the evidential burdens) described in relation to section 25 apply to this section too (*subsections (1)(d) and (e), (2) and (3)*). Whether or not the child consented to the incitement, or the activity being incited is irrelevant.

Section 27: Family relationships

55. Section 27 lists the relationships relevant for the purposes of sections 25 and 26. Section 67 of the Adoption and Children Act 2002 provides that an adoptive child is the child of the adoptive parents and not the biological parents. Adoptive relationships are therefore covered by *subsection (1)(a)*. The categories at *subsections (2)* to *(4)* also apply (by virtue of *subsection (1)(b)*) to the adoptive child's biological family relationships. These relationships fall into three categories.

56. The first category of relationships is listed in *subsection (2)*. Definitions of the relationships mentioned at subsection (2) are at *subsection (5)(a)* to *(c)*. Persons whose relationships fall within this category will always be each other's family members for the purposes of sections 25 and 26. Even where there is no blood relationship and the relationship can therefore cease – as in the case of foster parents – this offence may be committed for as long as the victim is under 18. So for example even where A is no longer a child's foster parent, A will commit an offence by having sex with that child while the child is under 18.

57. The second category of relationships is listed in *subsection (3)*. The relationship between A and a child will only fall within this category for the purposes of sections 25 and 26 if A lives, or has lived, in the same household as the child <u>or</u> is, or has been, regularly involved in caring for, training or supervising or being in sole charge of the child. *Subsection (3)(a)* relates to step-parents, *(3)(b)* relates to cousins, *(3)(c)* relates to step-siblings and *(3)(d)*

relates to foster-siblings. The definition of foster parent is at *subsection (5)(c)* and the definition of step-parent, stepbrother and stepsister is at *subsection (5)(e)*. An example within this category would be a person (A) who lives or has lived in the same house as his first cousin who is under 18. If the cousins had never lived in the same household, A would not commit this offence by having a sexual relationship with the cousin. As with the first category, if the relationship ceases (for example A ceases to be the partner of the child's mother), the offence will still be committed if A has sex with the child while the child is under 18.

58. An example of the third category of relationships (at *subsection (4)*) would be where a child is living in the same household as an au pair who looks after him. This category of relationship differs from the other two categories in that an offence will not be committed if A has a sexual relationship with the child after the relationship has ceased, even where the child is under 18. So, in this example, if the au pair were to leave the household and/or cease to have responsibility for the child, then the relationship would no longer be relevant for the purposes of sections 25 or 26

Section 28: Sections 25 and 26: marriage exception

59. This section provides A with a defence to the offences under sections 25 and 26 if he can prove that at the time of the act the child was aged 16 or over and he was lawfully married to the child.

Section 29: Sections 25 and 26: sexual relationships which pre-date family relationships

60. This section provides A with a defence to the offences under sections 25 and 26 if he can prove that his sexual relationship with the child pre-dated the start of the familial relationship as defined in section 27. Thus, for example, where two divorced people meet because their respective 16 and 17 year old children are engaged in a sexual relationship and the parents decide to marry, if all four persons were to move into the same household the criminal law would not interfere in the ongoing sexual relationship between the children, even though they would otherwise have been brought within the scope of the offence. This defence is not available where A and the child are related as set out in section 27(2) (whether by blood or adoption). The effect of *subsection (2)* is to limit this to the situation where the sexual relationship was lawful so it would not cover for example a relationship with a child of under 16.

Section 30: Sexual activity with a person with a mental disorder impeding choice

Section 31: Causing or inciting a person, with a mental disorder impeding choice, to engage in sexual activity

Section 32: Engaging in sexual activity in the presence of a person with a mental disorder impeding choice

Section 33: Causing a person, with a mental disorder impeding choice, to watch a sexual act

61. All the offences in these sections are concerned with the situation where a person (A) involves another person (B) in sexual activity where B has a mental disorder and because of that mental disorder, or for reasons related to it, B is unable to refuse involvement in the sexual activity. "Mental disorder" is stated at section 79(6) to have "the meaning given by section 1 of the Mental Health Act 1983". In section 1(2) of that Act, subject to section 1(3),

mental disorder is defined as "mental illness, arrested or incomplete development of mind, psychopathic disorder and any other disorder or disability of mind." A person with a "learning disability" would fall within this definition. The definition of sexual activity is at section 78. *Subsection (2)* of each section contains a definition of what is meant by B being unable to refuse.

62. The offences are divided according to the different types of sexual activity (the types of sexual activity covered are the same as for the child sex offences (sections 9 to 12)).

63. Section 30 covers touching, which as section 79(8) explains, includes any type of physical contact including penetration.

64. Section 31 covers the situation where A causes or incites B to engage in sexual activity, for example, where A causes B to have sexual intercourse with A's friend, or incites him to do so, even if the incitement does not result in B engaging in sexual activity.

65. Section 32 covers the situation where, for the purpose of obtaining sexual gratification, A engages in sexual activity in the presence of B, or in a place from which B can observe him. The offence is only committed, however, where A knows or believes that B is aware of the sexual activity or intends him to be aware of it. B might be aware of the sexual activity because he is watching it at A's behest or because A is describing what he is doing to B.

66. Section 33 covers the situation where A, for his sexual gratification, causes B to watch a third person engaging in sexual activity or to look at an image of a person engaging in sexual activity. "Image" is defined in section 79(4)).

Section 34: Inducement, threat or deception to procure sexual activity with a person with a mental disorder

Section 35: Causing a person with a mental disorder to engage in or to agree to engage in sexual activity by inducement, threat or deception

Section 36: Engaging in sexual activity in the presence, procured by inducement, threat or deception, of a person with a mental disorder

Section 37: Causing a person with a mental disorder to watch a sexual act by inducement, threat or deception

67. Like the previous set of offences, these sections are concerned with the situation where a person (A) involves another person (B) in sexual activity where B has a mental disorder. However, for these offences, there is no need to prove that B is unable to refuse. Instead, the offences address the situation where A uses inducements, threats or deceptions to obtain B's agreement to the sexual activity. The definition of mental disorder is at section 79(6); the definition of sexual activity is at section 78. An inducement might be A promising B presents of anything from sweets to a holiday; a threat might be A stating that he will hurt a member of B's family; and a deception might be A stating that B will get into trouble if he does not engage in sexual activity, or persuading him that it is expected that friends should engage in sexual activity. The division of the sections according to the type of sexual activity involved is similar to that in the previous set of offences.

Section 38: Care workers: sexual activity with a person with a mental disorder

Section 39: Care workers: causing or inciting sexual activity

Section 40: Care workers: sexual activity in the presence of a person with a mental disorder

Section 41: Care workers: causing a person with a mental disorder to watch a sexual act

68. Like the previous two sets of offences, these sections are concerned with the situation where a person (A) involves another person (B) in sexual activity where B has a mental disorder. The difference here is that A and B must be in a relationship of care. There is no need to prove that B is unable to refuse. The definition of mental disorder is at section 79(6); the definition of sexual activity is at section 78. The relationships of care that are covered by these offences are set out at section 42. The offences are divided according to the different types of sexual activity involved. The division is the same as for sections 30 to 33 and what is said in the notes for those sections about the different types of sexual activity covered applies here too. The prosecution must prove, in addition to the other requirements, that the defendant knew or could reasonably have been expected to know that B had a mental disorder. *Subsection (2)* of each section puts an evidential burden on A in this respect. This means that, unless A shows from the evidence that there is an arguable case as to whether or not he knew or could reasonably have been expected to know of B's mental disorder, it is presumed that he did know or could reasonably have been expected to know of this.

Section 42: Care workers: interpretation

69. This section defines a relationship of care for the purposes of sections 38 to 41. An example of a relationship covered by *subsection (2)* is where A is a member of staff in a care home and B is a resident there. An example of a relationship covered by *subsection (3)* is where A is a receptionist at the clinic that B attends every week. *Subsection (4)* covers any situation where A provides care, assistance or services to B in connection with B's mental disorder. An example of a relationship covered by *subsection (4)* is where A takes B on outings every week or treats B for his learning disability with complementary therapies in B's own home. In all cases, A must have, or be "likely to have", regular face to face contact with B. The "likely to have" limb is to cover persons who provide care to B in these situations from day one of their involvement with B.

Section 43: Sections 38 to 41: marriage exception

70. This section provides A with a defence to the offences under sections 38 to 41 if he proves he was lawfully married to B at the time of the sexual activity and B was over 16.

Section 44: Sections 38 to 41: sexual relationships which pre-date care relationships

71. This section provides A with a defence to the offences under sections 38 to 41 if he proves that his sexual relationship with B pre-dated his relationship of care with B. But the sexual relationship must have been lawful for this defence to apply. So if A and B had a lawful sexual relationship before B developed his mental disorder and A started caring for him, A would not commit an offence by continuing that sexual relationship.

Section 45: Indecent photographs of persons aged 16 or 17

72. This clause redefines a "child" for the purposes of the Protection of Children Act 1978 ("the 1978 Act") as a person under 18 years, rather than under 16 years, of age. This change means the offences under that Act of taking, making, permitting to take, distributing, showing, possessing with intent to distribute, and advertising indecent photographs or

pseudo-photographs of children will now also be applicable where the photographs concerned are of children of 16 or 17 years of age. The same change applies to the offence of possessing an indecent photograph or pseudo-photograph of a child at section 160 of the Criminal Justice Act 1988 (section 160(4) applies the 1978 Act definition of "child").

73. However, the clause also creates a number of conditions which if satisfied will mean that the defendant is not guilty of an offence under section 1(1)(a), (b) or (c) of the 1978 Act (provided that the offence charged relates to a photograph and not a pseudo-photograph).

74. The conditions in relation to an offence under section 1(1)(a) of the 1978 Act (taking or making indecent photographs) are as follows:

75. Firstly, the defendant must prove that the photograph in question was of the child aged 16 or over and that at the time of the taking or making of the photograph he and the child were married or living together as partners in an enduring family relationship (section 1A(1)).

76. Secondly, the defendant must show that there is enough evidence to raise an issue as to whether the child consented to the photograph being taken or made, or as to whether the defendant reasonably believed that the child consented (section 1A(4)).

77. Thirdly, the photograph must not be one that shows a person other than the child and the defendant (section 1A(3)).

78. If any of these conditions is not satisfied, the prosecution need only prove the offence as set out in section 1(1)(a) of the 1978 Act. But if the three conditions are satisfied, the defendant is not guilty of the offence unless the prosecution also prove that the child did not consent and that the defendant did not reasonably believe that the child consented (section 1A(4)).

79. The conditions in relation to an offence under section 1(1)(b) of the 1978 Act (distributing or showing indecent photographs) are as follows;

80. Firstly, the defendant must prove that the photograph in question was of the child aged 16 or over, and that either at the time of distributing or showing it, or at the time of obtaining it, he and the child were married or living together as partners in an enduring family relationship (section 1A(1) and (2)).

81. Secondly, the photograph must not be one that shows a person other than the child and the defendant (section 1A(3)).

82. If either of these conditions is not satisfied, the prosecution need only prove the offence as set out in section 1(1)(b) of the 1978 Act. But if both the conditions are satisfied, the defendant is not guilty of the offence unless the prosecution prove that the showing or distribution was to a person other than the child (section 1A(5)).

83. The conditions in relation to an offence under section 1(1)(c) of the 1978 Act (being in possession of indecent photographs with a view to their being distributed or shown) are as follows:

84. Firstly, the defendant must prove that the photograph in question was of the child aged 16 or over and that either at the time of his possession of it with a view to distributing or showing it, or at the time when he obtained it, he and the child were married or living together as partners in an enduring family relationship (section 1A(1) and (2)).

85. Secondly, the defendant must show that there is enough evidence to raise an issue as to whether the child consented (or the defendant reasonably believed that the child consented) to the photograph's being in the defendant's possession, and also as to whether the defendant had the photograph in his possession with a view to distributing or showing it to a person other than the child (section 1A(6)).

86. Thirdly, the photograph must not be one that shows a person other than the child and the defendant (section 1A(3)).

87. If any of these conditions is not satisfied, the prosecution need only prove the offence as set out in section 1(1)(c) of the 1978 Act. But if the three conditions are satisfied, the defendant is not guilty of the offence unless the prosecution also prove either that the child did not so consent and that the defendant did not reasonably believe that the child so consented, or that the defendant had the photograph in his possession with a view to its being distributed to a person other than the child.

88. Similar provision is made in relation to an offence under section 160 of the Criminal Justice Act 1988 (possession of indecent photograph of a child). The conditions are as follows:

89. Firstly, the defendant must prove that the photograph in question was of the child aged 16 or over and that at the time when he possessed the photograph, or at the time when he obtained it, he and the child were married or living together as partners in an enduring family relationship (section 160A(1) and (2)).

90. Secondly, the defendant must show that there is enough evidence to raise an issue as to whether the child consented to the photograph being in his possession or as to whether the defendant reasonably believed that the child so consented (section 160A(4)).

91. Thirdly, the photograph must not be one that shows a person other than the child and the defendant (section 160A(3)).

92. If any of these conditions is not satisfied, the prosecution need only prove the offence as set out in section 160 of the Criminal Justice Act 1988. But if the three conditions are satisfied, the defendant is not guilty of the offence unless the prosecution prove that the child did not consent and that the defendant did not reasonably believe that the child consented (section 160A(4)).

Section 46: Criminal proceedings, investigations etc.

93. This clause creates a limited defence to the offence of "making" an indecent photograph or pseudo-photograph of a child, under section 1(1)(a) of the Protection of Children Act 1978. "Making" covers, for example, the situation where a person downloads an image from the Internet or copies a computer hard drive. The defence applies where a person "making" such a photograph or pseudo-photograph can prove that it was necessary for him to do so for the purposes of the prevention, detection or investigation of crime, or for the purposes of criminal proceedings. The defence also applies to a member of the Security Service or GCHQ (Government Communications Headquarters) who can prove that it was necessary for him to "make" the photograph or pseudo-photograph for the exercise of the functions of the Security Service or GCHQ.

Section 47: Paying for sexual services of a child

94. Section 47 makes it an offence for any person (A) intentionally to obtain for himself the sexual services of a child (B) aged under 18, where those services have been paid for or where payment has been promised. The offence covers the situation where A pays for the services or promises payment either directly to B or to a third party (C) (for example where C is B's pimp) or where A knows that another person (D) has paid for the services or promised such payment. Where B is 13 or over, the offence will not be committed where A reasonably believes that B is 18 or over. (It will be for the prosecution to prove that A does not reasonably believe that B is 18 or over) However, where B is under 13, A will commit the offence regardless of any reasonable belief he may have about B's age. *Subsection (2)* defines payment widely. It covers not only a payment of money but any financial advantage. This includes the discharge of an obligation to pay (for example, B owes A a debt for a car but A agrees to waive the debt if B provides him with sexual services) and the provision of goods or services gratuitously or at a discount (for example, where A provides drugs to B at no or reduced cost on condition that B provides sexual services to A).

Section 48: Causing or inciting child prostitution or pornography

95. Section 48 makes it an offence for a person (A) intentionally to cause or incite a child under 18 (B) into prostitution or involvement in pornography anywhere in the world. The offence is aimed at persons who recruit into prostitution or pornography (whether on a one-off basis or longer term) those who are not involved or not currently involved in it. This could be where A makes a living from the prostitution of others and encourages new recruits to work for him or another (whether those recruits do actually then engage in prostitution or not). It could also cover the situation where A and B live together and A compels B to become involved in pornography, for example in order to pay their rent, or for any other reason. Unlike the prostitution offence at section 53, there is no requirement that the causing or inciting of a child prostitute must be done for gain. The prostitution or pornography can take place, or be intended to take place, in any part of the world. Where B is 13 or over, the offence will not be committed where A reasonably believes that B is 18 or over. (It will be for the prosecution to prove that A does not reasonably believe that B is 18 or over). However, where B is under 13, A will commit the offence regardless of any reasonable belief he may have about B's age. The terms "pornography" and "prostitute" are defined in section 51.

Section 49: Controlling a child prostitute or a child involved in pornography

96. Section 49 makes it an offence for a person (A) intentionally to control any of the activities of a child (B) that relate to the child's prostitution or involvement in pornography in any part of the world. The offence is committed even if B's activities in relation to prostitution or pornography are controlled for part of the time by another person. An example of the behaviour that might be caught by this offence is where A requires or directs B to charge a certain price or to use a particular hotel for her sexual services or to pose for a certain photographer and B complies with this request or direction. The prostitution or pornography can take place in any part of the world. Where B is 13 or over, the offence will not be committed where A reasonably believes that B is 18 or over. (It will be for the prosecution to prove that A does not reasonably believe that B is 18 or over). However, where B is under 13, A will commit the offence regardless of any belief he may have about B's age. The terms "pornography" and "prostitution" are defined in section 51.

Section 50: Arranging or facilitating child prostitution or pornography

97. Section 50 makes it an offence for a person (A) to arrange or facilitate the involvement of a child (B) in prostitution or pornography in any part of the world. This offence would cover for example, delivering B to a place where he will be used to make pornography or making arrangements for B's prostitution to take place in a particular room. Where B is 13 or over, the offence will not be committed where A reasonably believes that B is 18 or over. (It will be for the prosecution to prove that A does not reasonably believe that B is 18 or over). However, where B is under 13, A will commit the offence regardless of any reasonable belief he may have about B's age. The terms "pornography" and "prostitution" are defined in section 51.

Section 51: Sections 48 to 50: Interpretation

98. Section 51 defines the terms "pornography", "prostitute" and "prostitution" as used in sections 48 to 50.

Section 52: Causing or inciting prostitution for gain

99. Section 52 makes it an offence for a person (A) intentionally to cause or incite a person (B) into prostitution anywhere in the world where A does so for or in expectation of gain for himself or for a third party. Although this offence is not specifically limited to where B is aged 18 or over, it is aimed at cases where B is an adult, as the offence at section 48 specifically covers cases where B is under 18. Although prostitution by adults aged 18 or over is not an offence in itself, this offence is intended to cover those who, for gain, recruit others into prostitution, whether this be by the exercise of force or otherwise. The terms "prostitute" and "gain" are defined at section 54.

Section 53: Controlling prostitution for gain

100. Section 53 makes it an offence for a person (A) intentionally to control another person's activities relating to prostitution, in any part of the world, where A does so for, or in the expectation of, gain for himself or a third party. This offence covers the same behaviour as section 49, but is limited to prostitution. Although this offence is not specifically limited to cases where the person controlled is aged 18 or over, it is aimed at those cases, as the offence at section 49 specifically covers cases where the person controlled is under 18. The terms "prostitution" and "gain" are defined at section 54.

Section 54: Sections 52 and 53: interpretation

101. Section 54 provides definitions for the terms "gain", "prostitute" and "prostitution" as used in sections 52 and 53. Subsection (1) defines "gain" as any financial advantage, including the discharge of a debt or obligation to pay, or the provision of goods or services (including sexual services) for free, or at a discount. The reference to "sexual services" would cover someone who controls the activities of a number of women in prostitution, where the gain he derives from them is their engaging in sexual intercourse with him. It also covers the goodwill of any person likely to bring such a financial advantage. So in relation to the offence at section 52, for example, this would cover A inciting B to work as a prostitute for C, where A expects this will lead to C providing him (A) with cheap drugs at a later date. The definitions of "prostitute" and "prostitution" as used in sections 52 and 53 are those set out in section 51.

Section 55: Penalties for keeping a brothel used for prostitution

102. Section 55 amends the Sexual Offences Act 1956 to create a new offence of keeping a brothel used for prostitution. The new offence is triable either way with a maximum penalty on indictment of 7 years imprisonment.

Section 56: Extension of gender-specific prostitution offences

103. Section 56 introduces Schedule 1 (extension of gender-specific prostitution offences) to the Act. Schedule 1 widens the offences of "permitting the premises to be used for prostitution" (at section 35 of the Sexual Offences Act 1956), "loitering or soliciting for purposes of prostitution" and the provisions relating to cautions for this offence (at sections 1 and 2 of the Street Offences Act 1959), "kerb crawling" and "persistent soliciting of women for the purpose of prostitution" (at sections 1 and 2 of the Sexual Offences Act 1985), otherwise unchanged by this Act, to cover all people involved, irrespective of their gender.

Section 57: Trafficking into the UK for sexual exploitation

104. Section 57 makes it an offence for a person (A) intentionally to arrange or facilitate the arrival into the UK of a person (B), where A intends to do anything that would result in the commission of a relevant offence involving B, or believes that another person is likely to do something to, or in respect of, B that would result in the commission of a relevant offence involving B. In both cases, the relevant offence must take place after B's arrival in the UK but may take place anywhere in the world. "Relevant offence" is defined at *subsection (1)* of section 60.

105. This section re-enacts with amendments the offence in section 145 of the Nationality, Asylum and Immigration Act 2002.

106. A may intend the relevant offence to be committed, or believe that it is likely to be committed, in any part of the world. This is to ensure that an offence will be committed where, for example, A traffics B into the UK as an interim destination but intends to traffic B on to another country so he can be subjected to a sexual offence there.

107. A may intend to commit the relevant offence himself, or believe that another person will do so. So for example, it will be an offence for A to make arrangements to bring B into the UK believing that C will then, for gain, force B into prostitution in Germany (causing prostitution for gain will be a relevant offence). It is A's belief that is important, so the offence would still be committed if C never actually caused B to work as a prostitute.

108. A will only commit the offence if he intends that B should be the victim of an offence committed by A, or believes that B will be the victim of an offence committed by C. This will ensure that airline companies, road hauliers etc who are transporting someone without any such intent or belief are not captured. The offence is intended, however, to cover A if he is part of the enterprise of trafficking for sexual exploitation even if he is one link in a chain of people helping to traffic B. Provided A has the necessary intent or belief, the section will cover, for example, his recruiting B in B's country of origin, his making arrangements for transport and food for B's journey, his forging of immigration documents for B and his other involvement in bringing B to the UK.

Section 58: Trafficking within the UK for sexual exploitation

109. Section 58 makes it an offence for a person (A) intentionally to arrange or facilitate travel within the UK of a person (B) where A intends to do anything to, or in respect of, B

that would result in the commission of a relevant offence involving B, or where he believes that another person is likely to do something to, or in respect of, B that would result in the commission of a relevant offence involving B. In both cases, the relevant offence must take place during or after the journey but may take place anywhere in the world. "Relevant offence" is defined at *subsection (1)* of section 60. This offence is intended to apply both to UK nationals who are moved from one place to another in the UK to be sexually exploited as well as to others, including foreign nationals, who are, for example, trafficked to London from central Europe and then moved from London to another part of the UK to be sexually exploited.

Section 59: Trafficking out of the UK for sexual exploitation

110. Section 59 makes it an offence for a person (A) intentionally to arrange or facilitate the departure from the UK of a person (B) where A intends to do anything to, or in respect of, B that would result in the commission of a relevant offence involving B or A believes that another person is likely to do something to, or in respect of, B that would result in the commission of a relevant offence involving B. In both cases, the relevant offence must take place after B's departure and may take place anywhere in the world. "Relevant offence" is defined at *subsection (1)* of section 60

111. The offence is designed to cover the situation where B is in the UK, either because he is ordinarily resident here or because he has been trafficked here, but is then trafficked by A to another part of the world to be subjected to a sex offence.

Section 60: Sections 57 to 59: interpretation and jurisdiction

112. Section 60 gives, for the purposes of the above sections, the definition of "relevant offence". The definition includes acts done outside England and Wales and Northern Ireland which, if they had been done in either of those territories, would constitute an offence under Part 1 of the Bill or under section 1(1)(a) of the Protection of Children Act 1978 (or the equivalent offences in Northern Ireland). It is irrelevant for the purposes of this definition whether the act in question also constitutes an offence in the country in which it is carried out.

113. The section also defines the territorial extent and jurisdiction of the above sections. The offences will cover acts committed by any person in the UK. They will also cover acts committed outside the UK by any body incorporated under UK law such as a UK company, or by any of the categories of British person listed at *subsection (3)* of the section when abroad, irrespective of whether or not the act in question is a criminal offence under the law in the country in which it is committed.

Section 61: Administering a substance with intent

114. Section 61 makes it an offence for a person (A) intentionally to administer a substance or to cause any substance to be taken by another person (B) where A knows that B does not consent to taking that substance and where A intends to stupefy or overpower B so that any person can engage in sexual activity involving B.

115. The offence is intended to cover use of so-called "date rape drugs" administered without the victim's knowledge or consent, but would also cover the use of any other substance with the relevant intention. It would cover A 'spiking' B's drinks with alcohol

where B did not know he was consuming alcohol, but it would not cover A encouraging B to get drunk so that A could have sex with B, where B knew that he was consuming alcohol.

116. The substance may be administered to B in any way, for example, in a drink (as in the example given above), by injection or by covering B's face with a cloth impregnated with the substance.

117. The offence applies both where A himself administers the substance to B, and where A causes the substance to be taken by B, for example where A persuades a friend (C) to administer a substance to B, so that A can have sex with B, because C knows B socially and can more easily slip the substance into B's drink than A can.

118. However, the intended sexual activity need not involve A. In the example given above it could be intended that C or any other person would have sex with B.

119. The term "sexual", used in this section in the phrase "sexual activity", is defined in section 78. The sexual activity in this offence could involve A having sexual intercourse with or masturbating B; could involve A causing B to commit a sexual act upon himself (for example, masturbation); or could involve B and a third party engaging in sexual activity together, regardless of whether the third party had administered the substance.

120. The offence would be made out where A administers the substance or causes B to take it (with the relevant intent) regardless of whether any sexual activity took place, for example because a friend of B saw what was happening and intervened to protect B.

Section 62: Committing an offence with intent to commit a sexual offence

121. Section 62 makes it an offence for a person (A) intentionally to commit any criminal offence with intent to commit any relevant sexual offence as defined in *subsection (2)*. This offence is intended to capture the situation where A commits a criminal offence but does so with the intention of committing a subsequent sexual offence, regardless of whether or not the substantive sexual offence is committed. It would apply, for example, where A kidnaps B so that he can rape him but is caught by the police before committing the rape. It would also apply where A detained B in his flat with this intention, or assaulted B to subdue him so that he could more easily rape him. If A does commit the intended offence, he could be charged with the substantive sexual offence in addition to this offence.

Section 63 Trespass with intent to commit a sexual offence

122. Section 63 makes it an offence for A to intend to commit a "relevant sexual offence" (defined at *subsection (2)* of section 62) whilst he is on any premises where he is a trespasser, either knowing, or being reckless as to whether, he is trespassing. A person is a trespasser if he is on any premises without the owner's or occupier's consent, or other lawful excuse. This offence is intended to capture, for example, the situation where a person (A) enters a building owned by B, or goes into B's garden or garage without B's consent, and he intends to commit a sexual offence against the occupier. The offence applies regardless of whether or not the substantive sexual offence is committed. A will commit the offence if he has the intent to commit a relevant sexual offence at any time while he is a trespasser. The intent is likely to be inferred from what the defendant says or does to the intended victim (if there is one) or from items in possession of the defendant at the time he commits the trespass (for example, condoms, pornographic images, rope etc.). A separate offence is needed to cover trespass (as opposed to relying on section 62) because trespass is a civil tort and not a criminal offence.

Section 64: Sex with an adult relative: penetration

Section 65: Sex with an adult relative: consenting to penetration

123. Section 64 makes it an offence for a person (A) aged 16 or over intentionally to penetrate sexually a relative (B) who is aged 18 or over if he knows or could reasonably have been expected to know that B is his relative. Section 65 makes it an offence for a person (A) aged 16 or over to consent to being penetrated sexually by a relative (B) aged 18 or over if he knows or could reasonably have been expected to know that B is his relative. For either offence to be committed the penetration must be "sexual", as defined at Section 78. This requirement ensures that penetration for some other purpose, for example where one sibling helps another to insert a pessary for medical reasons, is not caught by this offence. *Subsection (2)* of each section defines "relative" for the purposes of each offence.

124. Adoptive relatives are excluded from each offence. Paragraph 47 of Schedule 6 makes a consequential amendment to the Adoption and Children Act 2002, to the effect that the provision in the 2002 Act that makes an adoptive child a child of the adoptive parents does not apply in relation to these offences. So, for example, it will not be an offence under either of these sections for an adoptive brother and sister aged over 18 to have sexual intercourse.

125. The effect of *subsection (3)* of each section is that, unless A shows from the evidence that there is an arguable case as to whether or not he knew or could reasonably have been expected to know that B is his relative, it is presumed that he did know or could reasonably have been expected to know it.

Section 66: Exposure

126. Section 66 makes it an offence for a person intentionally to expose his genitals where he intends that someone will see them and be caused alarm or distress. It is not necessary for A's genitals to have been seen by anyone or for anyone to have been alarmed or distressed. For example, if a person exposes his genitals to some passers-by, he may (depending on his state of mind) commit the offence regardless of whether they actually see his genitals or whether they have been alarmed or distressed by seeing them.

Section 67: Voyeurism

127. Section 67 makes it an offence, under *subsection (1)* for a person, (A), to observe, for the purpose of his own sexual gratification, another person doing a private act, for instance by looking through a window or peephole at someone having sexual intercourse, where A knows the person observed does not consent to being looked at for this purpose.

128. *Subsection (2)* covers a person (A) operating equipment with the intention of enabling another person, for his sexual gratification, to observe a third person (B), doing a private act, where A knows that B does not consent to being so viewed. This would cover, for example, a landlord (A) operating a webcam to allow people on the internet for their sexual gratification to view live images of his tenant (B) getting undressed, if A knew that B did not consent to this.

129. *Subsection (3)* covers a person (A) recording another person (B) doing a private act with the intention of looking at the recording for his own sexual gratification, or intending other people to look, for their sexual gratification, at the recording, and where he knows that B does not consent to the recording of that act with that intention. This would therefore cover the person (A) who secretly films someone (B) masturbating in B's bedroom to show to

others for their sexual gratification. Proof that the intention was the sexual gratification of others could be derived from, for example, the fact that the image was posted on a pornographic website, or in a pornographic magazine. A will be caught by the offence whether or not those looking at the image know that the person filmed did not consent to being filmed with that intention.

130.   *Subsection (4)* would cover someone who, for example, drilled a spy-hole or installed a two-way mirror in a house with the intention of spying on someone for sexual gratification or allowing others to do so. A would be caught even if the peephole or mirror was discovered before it was used.

Section 68: Voyeurism: interpretation

131.   Section 68 defines "private act", and "structure" for the purposes of section 67.

Section 69: Intercourse with an animal

132.   Section 69 makes it an offence for a man intentionally to penetrate the vagina or anus of a living animal with his penis where he knows or is reckless as to whether that is what he is penetrating. The reference to vagina or anus in this context is further explained at *subsection (8)* of section 79. *Subsection (2)* of section 69 makes it an offence for a person intentionally to cause or allow her vagina or his or her anus to be penetrated by the penis of a living animal where he or she knows or is reckless as to whether that is what is doing the penetrating. This offence is related solely to penile penetration in relation to animals and does not replace existing legislation covering cruelty to animals.

Section 70: Sexual penetration of a corpse

133.   Section 70 makes it an offence for a person (A) intentionally to penetrate any part of the body of a dead person (B) with his penis, any other body part (for example his finger), or any other object, where that penetration is sexual. The offence is committed when A knows or is reckless as to whether he is penetrating any part of a dead body. This is intended to cover when A knows he is penetrating a dead body, for example in a mortuary, or where A is reckless as to whether B is alive or dead. It will not cover situations where A penetrates B fully believing B to be alive, but in fact B is dead, or where B unexpectedly dies during intercourse. The penetration must be sexual. A definition of sexual is given in section 78. This is to exclude legitimate penetration of corpses, for example that which occurs during an autopsy.

Section 71: Sexual activity in a public lavatory

134.   Section 71 makes it an offence intentionally to engage in sexual activities in a public lavatory. *Subsection (1)(a)* defines a public lavatory. The term "sexual" for the purposes of this clause is defined in *subsection (2)*. A definition distinct from that in section 78 is used in section 71 so as to include only sexual activities that a reasonable person would take to be sexual without knowledge of the purpose of the person carrying out the activity.

Section 72: Offences outside the United Kingdom

135. *Subsection (1)* of section 72 makes it an offence in England and Wales and Northern Ireland for a British citizen or UK resident (subject to *subsection (2)*) to commit certain acts overseas against a child under 16 (or, in Northern Ireland, under 17). The date referred to in *subsection (2)* is the commencement date of Part 2 of the Sex Offenders Act 1997, which this section re-enacts. The act done must amount to a sexual offence listed in Schedule 2 and must

also amount to an offence in the country where it was committed. The exact description of the offence does not need to be the same in both countries. For example, the provisions could apply to someone who raped a child in another country although that offence was described differently under the law in that country. *Subsection (4)* provides that the defendant can require the prosecution to prove that what was done was an overseas offence.

Section 73: Exceptions to aiding, abetting or counselling

136. Section 73 provides that, in certain defined circumstances, a person is not guilty of aiding, abetting or counselling a sexual offence under sections 5, 6 and 7 (offences against children under 13), section 9 (sexual activity with a child), section 13 (where the offence would be an offence under section 9 if the offender were over 18) and sections 16, 25, 30, 34 and 38 (where the victim is a child under 16).

137. The exception applies where the person is acting for the purpose of protecting a child from pregnancy or sexually transmitted infection, for the purpose of protecting the physical safety of a child, or for the purpose of promoting a child's emotional well-being. In this last case, however, the exception only applies where the person provides advice.

138. In all cases, the person must not be causing or encouraging the commission of an offence or a child's participation in it. Nor must the person be acting for the purpose of obtaining sexual gratification. So a person who was providing advice to a child under 16 about sexual health or contraception, in order to protect the child from becoming pregnant would not fall within the exception if he was at the same time meaning to encourage the child to have sex or was giving that advice in order to get sexual gratification for himself.

Section 74: "Consent"

139. Section 74 defines "consent" for the purposes of this Part. This definition is relevant to many sections in the Part including, for example, the offence of rape (section 1). The section refers to a person's capacity to make a choice. A person might not have sufficient capacity because of his age or because of a mental disorder.

Section 75: Evidential presumptions about consent

140. This section applies to the offences of rape (section 1), assault by penetration (section 2), sexual assault (section 3) and causing a person to engage in sexual activity without consent (section 4). The section provides for presumptions that may be challenged by the defendant. The presumptions arise in the circumstances described in *subsection (2)*. The difference between paragraphs (a) and (b) of *subsection (2)* is that paragraph (a) covers violence and threats of violence used against the complainant whereas paragraph (b) covers violence and threats of violence used against a person other than the complainant. The violence or threat must occur either at the time of the relevant act or immediately before it began.

141. The effect of *subsection (3)* is that where, for example, the relevant act for which the person is being prosecuted is penetration, but the penetration is the culmination of a series of sexual activities, then if the violence or threat occurred immediately before the first sexual activity (as opposed to before the penetration), the presumptions still arise.

142. Where the prosecution proves that the defendant did a relevant act (as defined in section 77), that the circumstances described in *subsection (2)* existed and that the defendant knew that those circumstances existed, the complainant will be presumed not to have consented to

the relevant act and the defendant will be presumed not to have reasonably believed that the complainant consented. In order for these presumptions not to apply, the defendant will need to satisfy the judge from the evidence that there is a real issue about consent that is worth putting to the jury. In practice (although this is not mentioned in the Act) the evidence produced may be from evidence that the defendant himself gives in the witness box, or from evidence given on his behalf by a defence witness, or resulting from evidence given by the complainant during cross-examination. If the judge is satisfied that there is sufficient evidence to justify putting the issue of consent to the jury, he will so direct; if not, he will direct the jury to find the defendant guilty.

Section 76: Conclusive presumptions about consent

143. This section creates conclusive presumptions about lack of consent and the absence of belief in consent in situations where the defendant deceived the complainant into sexual activity. *Subsection (2)(a)* covers the situation where, for example, the defendant intentionally tells the complainant that digital penetration of her vagina is necessary for medical reasons when in fact it is for his sexual gratification. *Subsection (2)(b)* covers the situation where, for example, the defendant impersonates the complainant's partner and thereby causes the complainant to consent to the relevant act. Where the prosecution prove that the defendant did a relevant act (as defined in section 77) and that any of the circumstances described in *subsection (2)* existed, it is conclusively presumed that the complainant did not consent to the relevant act and that the defendant did not believe that the complainant consented to the relevant act. The defendant will therefore be convicted.

Section 77: Sections 75 and 76: relevant acts

144. Section 77 defines the relevant acts to which the provisions in sections 75 and 76 apply.

Section 78: "Sexual"

145. Section 78 defines "sexual" for the purposes of this Part. This definition is relevant to many of the offences under this Part. For example, section 2(1)(b) refers to penetration which is sexual and section 3(1)(b) refers to touching which is sexual.

146. There are two alternative limbs to the definition of "sexual" in section 78. Paragraph (a) covers activity that the reasonable person would always consider to be sexual because of its nature, such as sexual intercourse. Paragraph (b) covers activity that the reasonable person would consider, because of its nature, may or may not be sexual depending on the circumstances or the intentions of the person carrying it out, or both: for example, digital penetration of the vagina may be sexual or may be carried out for a medical reason. Where the activity is, for example, oral sex, it seems likely that the reasonable person would only need to consider the nature of the activity to determine that it is sexual. But where it is digital penetration of the vagina, the reasonable person would need to consider the nature of the activity (it may or may not be sexual), the circumstances in which it is carried out (eg a doctor's surgery) and the purpose of any of the participants (if the doctor's purpose is medical, the activity will not be sexual; if the doctor's purpose is sexual, the activity also is likely to be sexual).

147. If, from looking at the nature of the activity, it would not appear to the reasonable person that the activity might be sexual, the activity does not meet the test in either paragraph (a) or (b), even if a particular individual may obtain sexual gratification from carrying out the

activity. The effect of this is that obscure fetishes do not fall within the definition of sexual activity.

Section 79: General interpretation

148. Section 79 gives a number of definitions relevant to offences in this Part. *Subsection (2)* is needed so that where, for example, a person consents at the time of entry to penetration, but then withdraws his consent and the penetration continues, the person penetrating may be guilty of rape or assault by penetration.

Part 2: Notification and Orders

Section 80: Persons becoming subject to notification requirements

149. Sections 80 to 92 re-enact, with amendments, Part 1 of the Sex Offenders Act 1997(the 1997 Act), which established a requirement on sex offenders to notify certain personal details to the police. This process is commonly known as "registration", and often referred to loosely as creating a "sex offenders' register". Sections 80 and 81 set out the persons who are required to comply with the notification requirements. Such a person is referred to as a "relevant offender" (*subsection (2)*).

150. *Subsection (1)* provides that notification requirements apply to a person who is dealt with by a court, in any of the ways specified in the subsection (which include conviction), in respect of an offence specified in Schedule 3.The offences in Schedule 3 are exclusively sexual offences, and include the offences that were listed in the corresponding section of Schedule 1 of the 1997 Act. In relation to England, Wales and Northern Ireland, Schedule 3 also includes various offences under Part 1 of this Act. A number of the offences in Schedule 3 are subject to age and sentence thresholds beneath which the offence will not trigger the notification requirements.

151. In relation to section 80 (and Part 2 generally) a "conviction" includes a conviction after commencement which results in a conditional but not an absolute discharge: section 134 provides that in relation to an order for a conditional discharge, the legislation that deems a conviction with an absolute or conditional discharge not to be a conviction, does not apply in relation to this Part of the Act. The term "convicted" as it applies to mentally disordered offenders is explained at section 135(1) and (2). The reference at *subsection (1)(c)* is further explained at section 135(3).

152. *Subsection (1)(d)* refers to a person who is cautioned for a relevant offence. Section 133 provides that the term "caution" includes a reprimand or warning given under section 65 of the Crime and Disorder Act 1998 (the 1998 Act). These reprimands and warnings are given to young offenders.

Section 81: Persons formerly subject to Part 1 of the Sex Offenders Act 1997

153. Section 81 provides that, on commencement of this Part of the Act, offenders previously subject to the notification requirements of the 1997 Act by virtue of a conviction, relevant finding or caution for an offence listed in Schedule 3 of this Act, will be subject to the notification requirements of this Part unless their period of notification ended before commencement. *Subsections (3)* to *(6)* replicate the partially retrospective provisions of the 1997 Act, so that, save in specified circumstances, convictions, findings and cautions that pre-date 1 September 1997 (the date of commencement of the 1997 Act) will not trigger the notification requirements. *Subsections (7)* and *(8)* relate to persons who immediately before

commencement of this Part were subject to a sex offender order or an interim sex offender order in England, Wales, Northern Ireland or Scotland, or a restraining order in England and Wales. These orders all impose the notification requirements under the 1997 Act. Such persons will, from commencement, become subject to the notification requirements of this Part of this Act until the order ceases to have effect.

Section 82: The notification period

154. Section 82 sets out the period during which a relevant offender will be subject to the notification requirements. In the most serious cases, as reflected in the sentence passed for the offence, the person will be subject to the requirements for an indefinite period, which means the rest of his life. In less serious cases, the offender will be subject to the requirements for a fixed period. For example, where after commencement a person is cautioned for a relevant offence, the notification period is two years.

155. The notification period starts from the date of conviction, finding or caution. This is called the 'relevant date' (*subsection (6)*). The 'relevant date' in relation to offences in Schedule 3 that are subject to sentence thresholds is set out in section 132.

156. *Subsection (2)* provides that, where an adult would be subject to the notification requirements for a determinate period (that is ten, seven, five or two years), that period will be halved in the case of an offender who is under 18 on the relevant date (that is, the date of conviction, relevant finding or reprimand or final warning).

157. *Subsections (3)* and *(4)* set out how to calculate the notification period where an offender is sentenced for more than one Schedule 3 offence and these sentences are terms of imprisonment running consecutively or partly concurrently. Where the terms are consecutive, they are to be added together. For example, where an offender is sentenced to 3 months' imprisonment for one relevant offence and 10 months' imprisonment for another such offence, to run consecutively, the sentence would be treated as 13 months' imprisonment for the purposes of working out the notification period (in this case, 10 years). Terms will be partly concurrent when they are imposed on different occasions. An example would be where an offender is sentenced to 10 years' imprisonment for a Schedule 3 offence, and 6 years into this term he is sentenced to 12 years' imprisonment for a second Schedule 3 offence. Where this is the case, the notification period is based on the combined length of the terms minus any overlapping period. In the example given, the combined length of the sentences would be 22 years and the overlapping period would be the remaining 4 years of the 10-year sentence. So the sentence for the purposes of working out the notification period would be 18 years.

158. *Subsection (5)* relates to the situation where there is an initial finding that a person is under a disability and has done the act charged and he is later tried for the offence. An example would be where such a finding was made, the person was admitted to hospital under a restriction order and the notification requirements would therefore apply for an indefinite period. Where such a person was subsequently tried for the offence, the indefinite notification period will cease to apply as from the end of the trial. If the person is convicted and sentenced to, say, 12 months' imprisonment for the offence, the new notification period would be 10 years, starting from the date of the conviction. If the person is acquitted at trial, the person ceases to be subject to the notification requirements in respect of that matter.

Section 83: Notification requirements: initial notification

159. Section 83 sets out the information the offender needs to supply to the police when he first makes a notification and the time scales within which he is required to provide that information.

160. *Subsection (2)* relates to a case where someone who is dealt with by a court in one of the ways specified at subsection 80(1) is, at the date of being so dealt with, already subject to the notification requirements by virtue of an earlier conviction or finding or caution in respect of a Schedule 3 offence., If, in these circumstances, at the date of being dealt with by the court, the person has complied with *subsection (1)* in respect of the earlier conviction or finding or caution, he does not need to notify his details again in accordance with *subsection (1)*. This is only the case, however, where the notification period in respect of the earlier conviction, finding or caution lasts throughout the period specified at *subsection (1)* (as extended in accordance with *subsection (6)* – see below – if appropriate).

161. *Subsection (4)* makes similar provision in respect of persons who are already subject to the notification requirements at the time when a notification order (as defined in section 97) is made.

162. *Subsection (3)* provides that the obligation imposed by *subsection (1)* does not apply to a person who, on commencement, in relation to a pre-commencement conviction, finding, caution or order, has complied with the obligation to notify his name and address to the police under section 2(1) of the 1997 Act. Where a person subject to the requirements of the 1997 Act has not complied with section 2(1) of that Act, he must, under *subsection (1)*, notify the police of the details in *subsection (5)* within 3 days of commencement of Part 2 of the Act.

163. The details in *subsection (5)* include the offender's home address. The term 'home address' is defined in *subsection (7)*. This provides that where an offender is homeless or has no fixed abode his 'home address' means an address or location where he can be regularly found. This might, for example, be a shelter, a friend's house, a caravan or a park bench.

164. In calculating the period within which an offender must give notification under *subsection (1)*, any time when the offender meets the conditions specified in *subsection (6)* - for instance, any time when he is serving a sentence of imprisonment - does not count.

Section 84: Notification requirements: changes

165. Section 84 sets out the requirements on a relevant offender to notify the police of changes to notified details. Under *subsection (1)(c)* an offender must notify the police within 3 days, of the address of any premises he has stayed at within the UK, besides his home address, for a 'qualifying period'. This place might be a friend or relative's house or a hotel where he has stayed. A qualifying period is defined at *subsection (6)* and is a period of 7 days, or two or more periods, in any twelve months, which taken together amount to 7 days.

166. *Subsection (2)* allows an offender to notify the police of any change to his notified details (his name, address or having stayed away from home for 7 or more days) in advance of such change. The advance notification must give a date when the change is expected to occur.

167. *Subsections (3)* and *(4)* deal with the scenario in which the change does not take place as notified in advance. As long as the change takes place no earlier than 2 days before the

date notified or no later than 3 days after the date notified, the offender need not update the police as to the actual date on which the change took place. However, where the change takes place outside this period, the person must notify the change in accordance with *subsection (1)*, that is, within 3 days of the actual change. And, where the change takes place 3 days or more after the date specified, the person must also notify the police (within 6 days of the date specified) that the information he notified in advance is no longer correct.

168. The effect of s*ubsection (5)* is that time when an offender is in custody, detained or abroad (as provided at *subsection (6)* of section 83), will be disregarded for the purpose of determining the 3 day period specified in *subsection (1)* and the 6 day period specified in *subsection (4)(b)*.

Section 85: Notification requirements: periodic notification

169. Section 85 provides (at *subsection (1)*) that an offender must re-notify the police of the details set out in *subsection (5)* of section 83 within one year after each of the specified events, unless during this period he re-notifies, because of a change of circumstances, under section 84.

170. The specified events are:

the commencement of this Part of the Act;

any notification the offender has given under *subsection (1)* of section 83 or 85; and

any earlier notification the offender has given under *subsection (1)*.

171. Commencement will only be a trigger for this periodic notification requirement where a person is exempt from complying with *subsection (1)* of section 83 by reason of *subsection (2), (3)* or *(4)* of section 83 (i.e., where the person has complied with an earlier initial notification requirement).

172. This means that where a person becomes subject to the notification requirements for the first time and does not change his name or address and does not stay away from home for 7 days or more, he will have to re-notify within a year of his initial notification and annually thereafter. Where a person does notify his having stayed away from home for 7 days, for example, he will have to re-notify the police of the information set out in *subsection (5)* of section 83 within a year of giving the notification of having stayed away from home. And, if within that year he notifies another period spent away from home, or a change of name or address, the re-notification of the details set out in section 83(5) will be put back to a year after that latter notification.

173. *Subsection (3)* provides that where a relevant offender is detained or abroad in the ways provided at *subsection (4)* at the time the periodic notification requirement falls due, the person may give that notification up to 3 days after he is released from the detention specified in *subsection (4)* or returns to the UK.

Section 86: Notification requirements: travel outside the United Kingdom

174. *Subsection (1)* of section 86 provides a power for the Secretary of State to make regulations setting out notification requirements for relevant offenders who leave the UK or for any description of such offenders (for example those intending to leave the UK for a specified period). The regulations would oblige such persons to notify certain details concerning their travel plans to the police.

175. *Subsection (4)* might be used for example to make provision for young offenders to notify for a different period of foreign travel than do other offenders

176. These regulations are subject to the affirmative resolution procedure (section 138(2)). For Scotland, the regulations will be made by Scottish Ministers and laid before the Scottish Parliament.

Section 87: Method of notification and related matters

177. Section 87 describes how and where an offender is required to notify information to the police under the sections relating to initial notification, change of details and periodic notification. It provides a power for the Secretary of State to make regulations specifying the police stations at which an offender may notify the police of the relevant information. For Scotland the regulations will be made by Scottish Ministers and laid before the Scottish Parliament. The regulations will prescribe one or more police stations for each police area and where more than one has been prescribed for a particular offender's area, that offender may notify at any one of them. The term 'local police area' is defined in *subsection (3)* of section 88. Where the notification relates to having stayed away from a home address for 7 days or more or to a prospective change of address, the offender may use a police station within the police area of that other address (*subsection (2)*). When making a notification, other than a notification of foreign travel, the police may take the person's fingerprints and/or a photograph (*subsection (4)*). The term "photograph" is explained at *subsection (2)* of section 88 and, because *subsection (4)(b)* of section 87 refers to a photograph of any part of the person, it will include an iris scan.

Section 88: Section 87: interpretation

178. *Subsection (3)* of section 88 defines "local police area". *Subsection 3(b)* and *(c)* deal with cases where the offender has no home address (as defined in *subsection (7)* of section 83). He may have no home address because for example he spends most of his time abroad and only returns to the UK occasionally, or because he is itinerant.

Section 89: Young offenders: parental directions

179. Section 89 provides that, in the case of a young offender, the court may direct a person with parental responsibility for the offender to comply with the notification requirements in place of the offender until either the offender attains the relevant age (18 in England, Wales and Northern Ireland and where the offender is dealt with by a service court; 16 in Scotland) or until an earlier date specified by the court. The court may make the direction at the time it deals with the offender in respect of an offence or finding which triggers the notification requirements, or when it makes an order which imposes those requirements. *Subsections (4)* and *(5)* also allow the police to apply to the court for a parental direction to be made. This will cover cases where the court, for whatever reason, did not make a direction at the stage referred to above but an order now seems appropriate. It will also cover cases where the young offender has received a reprimand or final warning for a Schedule 3 offence.

Section 90: Parental directions: variations, renewals and discharges

180. Section 90 provides that a court may vary, renew or discharge a parental direction. This may be required where, for example, there is a direction that the father notifies on behalf of the young offender and the father subsequently becomes divorced from the mother and the offender goes to live with the mother. Or an order may need to be discharged where, for

example, the parent can no longer control the young offender and is unable to ensure that he attends with the parent to notify. In these circumstances the court may consider that the liability for his failure to attend should revert to the young offender himself. *Subsections (2)(e)* and *(3)(a)* and *(b)* draw an explicit distinction between parental directions imposed by criminal courts and civil courts in Scotland in terms of the procedures and circumstances where such directions can be varied, renewed and discharged in Scotland.

Section 91: Offences relating to notification

181. *Subsection (3)* provides that the offence of failing to give a notification continues throughout the period during which the required notification is not given. An offender cannot be prosecuted more than once for the same failure. However, if an offender fails to comply with a requirement, is convicted for this offence and then fails to comply again in respect of the same requirement, he commits a new offence and may be prosecuted again.

182. An offence will not be committed where the person has a "reasonable excuse" for failure to comply with a notification requirement. This might be, for example, where an offender does not provide the information in the required time scale because he is in hospital following an accident. In respect of an offence relating to *subsection (2)(b)* of section 89 a reasonable excuse might be that the parent took all reasonable steps to persuade the young offender to accompany him to the police station.

Section 92: Certificates for the purposes of Part 2

183. Section 92 provides that when a court convicts or makes a relevant finding in respect of a person in relation to a Schedule 3 offence, or when a person is cautioned by the police, the court or police officer may issue a certificate that will be evidence of the conviction or finding or caution for a relevant offence and of the notification requirements which follow from it. *Subsection (4)* provides a power for the Secretary of State to prescribe by order the form certificate that will need to be issued by a police officer when a caution is given. These regulations will be subject to the negative resolution procedure (section 138(3)). Whilst the Regulations are in respect of cautions in England and Wales, a certificate made as a result of a caution will be sufficient evidence of that fact in a Scottish court.

Section 93: Abolished homosexual offences

184. Section 93 gives effect to Schedule 4 to the Act. Schedule 4 introduces a procedure whereby the Secretary of State may remove the notification requirement from offenders convicted of buggery and indecency between men (sections 12 and 13 of the Sexual Offences Act 1956) or convicted of attempting, inciting or conspiring to commit these offences or of aiding, abetting, counselling or procuring the commission of the offences. This procedure is necessary because in some cases, a man will be subject to the notification requirements in relation to consensual homosexual activity with a man who was aged 16 or over at the time of the offence.

Section 94: Part 2: supply of information to Secretary of State etc. for verification

185. Sections 94 and 95 provide the power to enable the police to verify that an offender has notified the correct details in compliance with sections 83, 84 and 85 of this Act or with the relevant sections of the Sex Offenders Act 1997, and that he is not omitting any details (such as another name or address he uses). This will be done by comparing the details provided at

notification against information the offenders will have provided to certain bodies performing Government functions.

186. *Subsection (3)* describes the police, and policing organisations having the power to supply this information. *Subsections (2) and (8)* describe the bodies to whom the information may be supplied. These are those bodies which perform social security, child support, employment and training functions on behalf of the Secretary of State for the Department of Work and Pensions (DWP) and the equivalent Northern Ireland Department, those who perform functions in relation to passports on behalf of the Home Secretary, and those who perform functions under Part 3 of the Road Traffic Act 1988 on behalf of the Secretary of State for the Department of Transport (i.e. the Driver and Vehicle Licensing Agency) or Part 2 of the Road Traffic (Northern Ireland) Order 1981. By virtue of *subsection (2)(c)*, section 94 also allows for the supply of information to persons providing services to the Secretary of State in connection with these functions i.e. an executive agency or private company.

187. By virtue of *subsection (1)*, the details the police may provide to these bodies are an offender's date of birth, national insurance number, any names he has notified, and his home address and any other addresses notified. This information may have been supplied by an offender at his initial notification, when notifying a change, or at his periodic notification.

188. *Subsection (4)* provides that this information may only be shared for the purpose of verifying that the information supplied to the police etc. by the offender is accurate and for the purpose of compiling a report of the comparison. It could not, for example, be used by DWP to pursue someone for a child support payment.

189. This section applies to Northern Ireland, the only difference being that the police may supply information to the Department for Social Development, the Department of the Environment or the Department for Employment and Learning in Northern Ireland or to a person providing services to these Departments in connection with a "relevant function".

190. *Subsection (6)* provides that any transfer of data must comply with the Data Protection Act 1998.

Section 95: Part 2: supply of information by Secretary of State etc.

191. Section 95 provides that the report complied under *subsection (4)(b)* of section 94 may be provided to the police (and the police organisations stated in *subsection (2)*). The police may retain the information and use it in the prevention, detection, investigation or prosecution of offences but for no other purpose. This would include an offence under section 91 of failing to comply with the notification requirements or by providing false information at notification (*Subsection (4)*). In addition, the information may be used to prevent, detect, investigate or prosecute other offences: for example, information that identified the possible whereabouts of an offender who was wanted for robbery could be used by the police in investigating that offence.

Section 96: Information about release or transfer

192. This section re-enacts, with amendments, section 5B of the 1997 Act. Section 96 allows the Secretary of State to make regulations requiring those who are responsible for an offender while he is in detention (as defined in *subsection (1)*) to notify other relevant authorities of his release or transfer to another institution. The regulations may define the person responsible for the offender (for example, the Chief Executive of a hospital) and the person

who must be informed about release and transfer. An example might be the governor of a prison being required to inform the local chief officer of police when a relevant offender is about to be released from his prison. These regulations will be subject to the negative resolution procedure (section 138(3)). For Scotland, the regulations will be made by Scottish Ministers and laid before the Scottish Parliament.

Section 97: Notification orders: applications and grounds

193. Section 97 provides a power for the police to apply to the magistrates' court for an order making an offender who has been convicted, cautioned or had a relevant finding made against him, in respect of a "relevant offence" (defined in *subsection (1)* of section 99) abroad, subject to the notification requirements.

194. The chief officer of police may apply for an order if the defendant resides in his police area or the chief officer believes that the person is currently in or is intending to come to his police area. The "intending to come to" limb will cover for example a person who is in France but who the chief officer of Kent believes has plans to arrive at Dover within the next few days. A notification order might, for example, be sought in respect of a UK citizen who has been convicted of a sexual offence overseas and who is deported to the UK on release from prison abroad. The police could also apply for a notification order in respect of a foreign citizen who the police know has been convicted of a sex offence in his or her own country and who comes to the UK.

195. The provisions in *subsection (3)* reflect the partially retrospective arrangements that apply in respect of the application of the notification requirements to people with convictions etc. in the UK (see section 81). The relevant conviction, finding or caution abroad must have taken place on or after 1 September 1997, which was the commencement date for the 1997 Act. Findings or convictions that occurred before that date will only be a trigger for a notification order where the person had yet to be dealt with on 1 September 1997 or was still serving a sentence or was subject to supervision or otherwise detained in respect of that offence on that date.

196. The effect of *subsection (4)* is that an order may not be made where the notification period (the period for which an offender is to be subject to the notification requirements), calculated from the date of conviction or finding or caution abroad, has expired. So where, for example, a person is cautioned abroad after commencement for a relevant offence (the notification period for a post-commencement caution is 2 years), the court may not make a notification order against that person if he comes to the UK more than 2 years after receiving the caution. Clause 103 provides certain modifications to clause 99 to ensure that the provisions contained therein reflect Scottish procedures, practices and references.

Section 98: Notification orders: effect

197. Section 98 provides that where an order is made, the offender will become subject to the notification requirements for the period set out in section 82 that applies to the sentence he received abroad. This period will run from the date of conviction or finding or caution abroad. So for example, if a person was convicted abroad of an offence equivalent to the domestic offence of sexual assault and sentenced to 6 months' imprisonment, the notification period for the sentence of 6 months would be 7 years. If the offender did not come to the UK until 5 years after the conviction, the notification requirements imposed under a notification order would only last for the remaining 2 of the 7 years since the date of conviction.

198. The provisions of *subsection (3)* modify the notification provisions as they apply to people subject to notification orders.

199. The effect of *subsection (4)* is that for people subject to notification orders, the initial obligation to provide details to the police will be within 3 days of the date of service of the order, and (subject to the other provisions in section 85 relating to annual notification) annually thereafter.

Section 99: Sections 97 and 98: relevant offences

200. A relevant offence for the purposes of a notification order is an act constituting an offence abroad, which would also have amounted to one of the offences set out in Schedule 3 had it been committed in the UK. The defendant may require the police to show that his offence if committed in the UK would have constituted an offence listed in Schedule 3. Otherwise, this is deemed to be accepted.

Section 100: Interim notification orders

201. Section 100 allows the police to apply for an interim notification order pending the application for a main order being heard. This may be, for example, because papers need to be obtained from a foreign country before the main application for a notification order can be determined. *Subsections (5)* and *(6)* provide that the offender will be subject to the notification requirements during the period of the interim notification order, with the notification period starting from the date of service of the order, as opposed to the date of the conviction etc. This means, for example, that the defendant will have to comply with the initial notification requirement (at section 83(1)) within 3 days of the service of the order, unless the period for compliance is extended to take into account any period during which the offender meets the conditions set out in section 83(6).

Section 101: Notification orders and interim notification orders: appeals

202. Section 101 allows the offender to appeal to the Crown Court against the making of an interim or full notification order.

Section 102: Appeals in relation to notification orders and interim notification orders: Scotland

203. Section 102 allows the offender to appeal against the making of an interim or full notification order in accordance with normal civil procedures. It also makes clear that where an appeal has been taken against an interlocutor any order can continue to have effect pending the appeal.

Section 103: Sections 97 to 100: Scotland

204. Section 103 applies the notification order power to Scotland, subject to certain modifications. The procedure for the notification order mirrors the existing procedure for sex offender orders, so these modifications ensure that the procedure is consistent with this and with Scottish civil procedure. The police will apply for a notification order by summary application and a record of evidence is required to be kept by the clerk. This procedure is similar to that required for sex offender orders.

Section 104: Sexual offences prevention orders: applications and grounds

205. Section 104 states the circumstances in which a sexual offences prevention order may be made against an offender. Sexual offences prevention orders are civil preventative orders

designed to protect the public from serious sexual harm. These orders replace, with amendments, restraining orders and sex offender orders (provisions in relation to which are found at section 5A of the 1997 Act and sections 2 to 4 and section 20 of the 1998 Act respectively in relation to England, Wales and Scotland, and at Article 6 and 6A of the Criminal Justice (Northern Ireland) Order 1998).

206. A court may make a sexual offences prevention order:

> when it deals with a person in respect of an offence listed at Schedule 3 or Schedule 5 to the Act, or, in the case of a mentally incapacitated offender, deals with him in respect of a finding relating to such an offence; or

> (in the case of a magistrates' court) when an application for such an order is made to it by a chief officer of police in respect of a person, and it is satisfied that:

> the person has been dealt with by a court in respect of an offence listed in Schedule 3 (other than at paragraph 60) or at Schedule 5; or has been dealt with by a court abroad in respect of an act which was an offence under the law of that territory and which would, if committed in any part of the UK, have constituted an offence listed in Schedule 3 (other than at paragraph 60) or at Schedule 5; and that

> the person's behaviour, since the date on which he was first dealt with in this way, means it is necessary to make the order "for the purpose of protecting the public or any particular members of the public from serious sexual harm from the offender".

207. A chief officer of police may only make an application to a magistrates' court as described above if two conditions are met. These conditions are:

> that the person has been dealt with in respect of an offence listed at Schedule 3 (other than at paragraph 60 of that Schedule) or at Schedule 5, or has been dealt with abroad in respect of an act which constituted an offence under the law of the territory in question, and which would, if committed in the UK, have constituted an offence listed at Schedule 3 (other than at paragraph 60) or at Schedule 5; and

> that the person's behaviour, since the first date on which he was dealt with in this way (this will be relevant if for example an offender has been convicted of several offences listed in Schedule 3), gives rise to reasonable cause to believe that it is necessary for such an order to be made.

208. The offences in Schedule 3 are all sexual offences, some of which are subject to thresholds in relation to age and sentence, below which the offence will not trigger a sexual offences prevention order. The offences in Schedule 5 are violent offences and various offences under this Act relating to trafficking and prostitution and child pornography. Schedule 5 includes murder as well as all the offences in Schedule 15 of the Criminal Justice Act 2003, which relates to the provisions in that Act dealing with "dangerous offenders".

209. In its application to Scotland, section 104 essentially allows a chief constable to make an application for such an order in respect of persons convicted in the UK of a sexual offence set out in Schedule 3 (other than at paragraph 60 of that Schedule) or, where the person has a conviction from England, Wales or Northern Ireland, in respect of offences set out in paragraphs 1 to 63 of Schedule 5.

210. The term "protecting the public in the United Kingdom or any particular members to the public from serious sexual harm from the defendant" is defined in *subsection (3)* of

section 106. The court may be satisfied of this necessity either by the circumstances of the offence or from other evidence of the defendant's behaviour.

211. An example of when the police might apply for a sexual offences prevention order is as follows. An offender has a conviction for sexual activity with a child and has been released after his term of imprisonment. Following his release he behaves in a way that suggests he is likely to offend again, for example by loitering around schools or inviting children back to his house. An application for a sexual offences prevention order is to be made by complaint. This is a civil procedure and the relevant procedure is set out at sections 51 to 57 of the Magistrates' Courts Act 1980.

Section 105: SOPOs: further provision as respects Scotland

212. Section 105 does not affect the power set out at section 104. But it makes further specific provision for a sheriff in Scotland to grant a sexual offences prevention order on the application of a chief constable in certain circumstances.

213. A chief constable may apply to a sheriff for an order under section 105 where he believes that a person is in, or is intending to come to the area of his police force, and that either:

> the person has been dealt with by a court in respect of an offence which comes within paragraph 60 of Schedule 3, in that in dealing with him, the court determined that there was a "significant sexual aspect" to his behaviour; or

> the person was dealt with by a court, before the commencement of this Part, in respect of an offence other than one listed at paragraphs 36 to 59 of Schedule 3, and it is likely that, had he been so dealt with after commencement, the court would have determined that his behaviour in committing the offence had a "significant sexual aspect; and

> that the person's behaviour, since he was dealt with in respect of the offence, has been such that there is reasonable cause to believe that such an order is necessary.

214. The sheriff may make an order under section 105 if he believes that it is necessary to do so to protect the public or any members of the public from serious sexual harm, and (in the case of a person who was dealt with in respect of an offence before the commencement of this Part) if he believes that there was a significant sexual aspect to the person's behaviour in committing the offence.

Section 106: Section 104: supplemental

215. *Subsection (5)* to *subsection (7)* define the term 'qualifying offender' which applies in relation to orders made against offenders living in the community. This includes those who have a conviction, finding or caution for an offence overseas that is equivalent to one of the offences in Schedules 3 or 5.

Section 107: SOPOs: effect

216. *Subsection (1)* of section 107 explains what an order does and for how long it lasts. An order may prohibit the offender from doing anything specified in it. *Subsection (2)* provides that the prohibitions contained within an order must be necessary "for the purpose protecting the public or any particular members of the public from serious sexual harm from the defendant". This phrase is defined in section 106(3). Prohibitions could include, for example,

preventing an offender from contacting his victims or from taking part in sporting activities that involve close contact with children or from living in a household with girls under 16.

217. The order must last for a minimum period of five years (*subsection 1(b)*). The period must be specified in the order but it may be an indefinite period and the period specified will not prevent a further order being made. However, *subsection (6)* operates to ensure an offender cannot be subject to more than one sexual offences prevention order at any one time.

218. *Subsection (3)* provides that where an order is made against an offender who is already subject to the notification requirements, but the notification period applicable to him would end during the currency of the order, he is to remain subject to the notification requirements for the duration of the order. If the notification period attaching to a relevant conviction, finding or caution lasts for longer than the order, the offender will remain subject to the notification requirements for that longer period.

219. *Subsection (4)* provides that where the offender is not subject to the notification requirements at the time an order is made, he will become subject to the notification requirements for the duration of the order.

220. The effect of *subsection (5)* is that the notification period runs from the date of service of the order (not from the date of the relevant conviction, caution or finding). This means, for example, that the defendant will have to comply with the initial notification requirement (at section 83(1)) within 3 days of the service of the order.

Section 108: SOPOs: variations, renewals and discharges

221. Section 108 enables either the offender subject to the order or the various chief officers of police listed in *subsection (2)* to apply for an order to be varied, renewed or discharged.

222. The defendant might, for example, seek to vary an order if he finds the prohibitions are operating on him unduly harshly. He might apply for a discharge if he intended to emigrate. A chief officer of police who believes the defendant is moving to his area might apply for a variation if, for example, the order was made when the defendant was living in another part of the country and only restricted the defendant's behaviour in that original area.

223. It may also be necessary to seek a renewal of an order at the time an existing order expires, where there is evidence that the defendant still requires the measures of restraint imposed in the original order.

224. *Subsection (8)* provides that the procedure in this section will apply where variations, renewals and discharges are sought in respect of restraining orders and sex offender orders made prior to the commencement of this Part of the Act.

Section 109: Interim SOPOs

225. Section 109 allows the police to apply for an interim sexual offences prevention order where an application has been made for a full order in respect of an offender living in the community. The purpose is to enable prohibitions to be placed on the offender's behaviour and to ensure that he will be subject to the notification requirements pending the application for the full order being determined. The interim order will be for a fixed period and will cease to have effect at the end of that period or, if earlier, when a decision is made on the full order.

226. The effect of *subsection (5)* is that the defendant will be subject to the notification requirements for the duration of the order, with the notification period to run from the date of service of the order. This means, for example, that the defendant will have to comply with the initial notification requirement (at section 83(1)) within 3 days of the service of the order.

Section 110: SOPOs and interim SOPOs: appeals

227. Section 110 provides for appeals against the making of an order or an interim order. The appeals process should be used where the offender is challenging the fact that an order has been imposed.

228. *Subsections (1)* and *(2)* explain the process by which an appeal should be brought depending on the circumstances in which the order was made. Where an order was imposed on the court's dealing with an offender for an offence listed in Schedule 3 or Schedule 5, the offender should follow the usual appeal process that would apply if he were appealing against sentence. So, where the order was made in the Crown Court, the appeal against the order should be made to the Court of Appeal. Where the order was made in the magistrates' court or the youth court, the appeal is to the Crown Court.

229. Where the order was made following an application by the police in respect of an offender in the community, the appeal will lie to the Crown Court.

230. *Subsection (5)* relates to orders made by the Crown Court following an appeal against an order imposed on an offender in the community. It provides that the order made by the Crown Court is to be treated as if it was made by the magistrates' court that imposed the original order, for the purposes of determining where any application for variation, renewal or discharge should be heard (under section 108 or 109).

Section 111: Appeals in relation to SOPOs and interim SOPOs: Scotland

231. Section 111 allows an offender in Scotland to appeal against the making of an interim or full order in accordance with normal civil procedures operating in Scotland. It also makes clear that where an appeal has been made the order can continue to have effect pending the appeal.

Section 112: Sections 104 and 106 to 109: Scotland

232. Section 112 sets out how sections 104 and 106 to 109 are to be read for Scotland. The effect is that the procedure for SOPOs in Scotland mirrors that for notification orders and foreign travel orders in Scotland. So the procedures are consistent with each other and with Scottish civil procedure. Accordingly, a chief constable will apply for a SOPO by summary application and a record of evidence will be required to be kept by the clerk.

Section 113: Offence: breach of SOPO or interim SOPO

233. Failure, without reasonable excuse, to comply with any prohibition in a sexual offences prevention order or an interim sexual offences prevention order is a criminal offence. Breach of any restraining order or sex offender order will also be an offence under this section.

Section 114: Foreign travel orders: applications and grounds

234. Section 114 provides for a new civil, preventative order, the foreign travel order. The foreign travel order will enable the courts to prohibit persons who are "qualifying offenders" (essentially, those dealt with in respect of certain sexual offences against a child under 16

(either in this country or abroad)) from travelling abroad where and so far as it is necessary to do so to protect a child or children from serious sexual harm outside the United Kingdom.

235. A foreign travel order may be made on application by the police to a magistrates' court and, if made, will place a prohibition on a sex offender from travelling abroad either to a named country or countries, to anywhere in the world other than a named country or to anywhere in the world.

236. The police may apply for a foreign travel order at the same time as a sexual offences prevention order or separately.

237. The term "qualifying offender" is defined at section 116. "Appropriate date" is defined in *subsection (5)* of section 115 and means the first date on which the offender was dealt with in respect of an offence in *subsection (1)* or (3) of section 116. The phrase "the purpose of protecting children generally or any child from serious sexual harm from the defendant outside the United Kingdom" is defined in section 115(2).

238. *Subsection (3)* sets out the circumstances in which the court may make an order.

Section 115: Section 114: interpretation

239. Section 115 defines certain terms used in section 114. *Subsection (6)* provides that, in the application of sections 115 and 116 to Northern Ireland, any reference to a child under 16 is to be taken to mean a child under 17.

Section 116: Section 114: qualifying offenders

240. Section 116 defines "qualifying offenders" for the purposes of a foreign travel order. *Subsection (1)* states that a "qualifying offender" is a person convicted of an offence listed at *subsection (2)*, or found not guilty of it by reason of insanity, or found to be under a disability and to have done the act charged in respect of it, or cautioned in respect of it..

241. *Subsection (2)(a)* lists a number of offences from Schedule 3 that deal with taking, making and distributing indecent photographs, or pseudo-photographs, of children under 16. *Subsection (2)(b)* refers to the offence of trespassing with intent to commit a sexual offence, where the intended offence was against a person under 16. *Subsection (2)(c)* refers to service offences which correspond to certain civilian sexual offences listed in Schedule 3. *Subsection (2)(d)* refers to an offence within any other paragraph of Schedule 3, where the victim was under 16.

242. *Subsection (3)* provides that a person also becomes a 'qualifying offender' if he is convicted of a 'relevant offence' committed outside the UK, or found not guilty of such an offence by reason of insanity, or found to have been under a disability and to have done the act charged in respect of such an offence, or cautioned in respect of such an offence. Whether he was so dealt with before or after the commencement of this Part of this Act is irrelevant.

243. A 'relevant offence' in this context is defined in *subsection (4)* as an act that was an offence in the country where it was committed, and which would have fallen within *subsection (2)* had it been committed in any part of the United Kingdom.

244. *Subsection (5)* provides that if the law of the foreign country in which an act is committed provides that it is to be punishable, then that act is an offence under the law of that country, however it is described in that law.

245. *Subsection (6)* and *subsection (7)* relate to the procedures to be adopted in satisfying the court that an act committed in a country other than the UK would have constituted an offence within *subsection (2)* if it had been done in any part of the UK. *Subsection (6)* provides that, unless the defendant serves a notice on the prosecution, (in the manner specified), requesting that the prosecution proves this to be the case, it will be assumed that the act would have constituted an offence within *subsection (2)* if done in any part of the UK. *Subsection (7)* permits the court to allow the defendant to require such proof from the prosecution even if he has failed to serve a notice as required by *subsection (6)*.

Section 117: Foreign travel orders: effect

246. Section 117 sets out the effect of a foreign travel order. *Subsection (1)* provides that the duration of the order will not exceed six months and will be specified in the order. *Subsection (2)* provides that the order may prohibit the subject from travelling to a country outside the UK named in the order (such as Thailand and Malaysia); or from travelling to any country outside the UK that is not named in the order (for example, this may be needed where the offender is banned from travelling anywhere in the world other than to a named country which he may need to visit for family reasons); or from travelling to any country outside the UK (where the offender is such a risk to children that a universal ban is required). *Subsection (4)* provides that if, while a foreign travel order is in force, the defendant is not a 'relevant offender' i.e. is not subject to the notification requirements of this Part of the Act, he must comply with any regulations made under section 86(1) (i.e. regulations imposing notification requirements relating to foreign travel). In practice, however, in the vast majority of cases the offender is likely already to be subject to all of the notification requirements by virtue of his conviction for a sexual offence against a child.

Section 118: Foreign travel orders: variations, renewals and discharges

247. Section 118 sets out provisions permitting the variation, renewal or discharge of a foreign travel order. A defendant may wish to apply for a variation of an order if for example the order prohibits him from travelling to Romania but during the course of the order he has to attend an urgent business meeting in Romania. The police may wish to apply for a renewal of an order if, on the expiry of the previous order, they still have cause to believe that the defendant poses a risk of serious sexual harm to children abroad. *Subsection (5)* provides that an application for variation, renewal or discharge may be made to the court which made the original order; or to a magistrates' court in the area where the subject of the order resides (this will probably generally be the case where the subject of the order is making the application); or to any magistrates' court in the police area of the chief officer making the application. *Subsection (3)* provides that the court that hears the application must hear any person mentioned in *subsection (2)* who wishes to be heard. Having done so, it may make any order it considers appropriate in the light of the restrictions in *subsection (4)*. *Subsection (4)* provides that any additional prohibitions imposed on the subject must be necessary for the purpose of protecting children generally or any child from serious sexual harm from the defendant.

Section 119: Foreign travel orders: appeals

248. This section provides a right of appeal to the Crown Court against the making of a foreign travel order. *Subsection (1)* provides that such an appeal may be against either the making of an order, or against the making of an order varying, renewing or discharging a foreign travel order, or against the refusal to make such an order. *Subsection (3)* provides that

any order made by the Crown Court, on an appeal against the making of a foreign travel order, will be deemed to be an order of the magistrates' court for the purposes of subsequent applications to vary, renew or discharge the order.

Section 120: Appeals in relation to foreign travel orders: Scotland

249. Section 120 sets out the appeals mechanism for such orders in Scotland. It also provides that during such an appeal the foreign travel order will remain in force.

Section 121: Sections 114 to 118: Scotland

250. This clause sets out the manner in which the foreign travel order regime is to apply in Scotland. The procedures for the foreign travel order mirror the proposed procedure for notification orders in Scotland so as to ensure that the procedures are consistent with each other and with Scottish civil procedure. Accordingly in *subsection (1)* the chief constable is required to apply for a foreign travel order by summary application.

Section 122: Offence: breach of foreign travel order

251. Section 122 makes it an offence for the offender to breach any prohibition contained within a foreign travel order without reasonable excuse. *Subsection (3)* provides that a court cannot make a conditional discharge (or a probation order in Scotland) where someone is convicted of this offence.

Section 123: Risk of sexual harm order: applications, grounds and effects

252. This and the following seven sections relate to a civil, preventative order for which the police can apply to a magistrates' court in respect of a person over the age of 18, if that person has on at least two occasions engaged in sexually explicit conduct or communication with a child or children, and as a result there is reasonable cause to believe that the order is necessary to protect a child or children from harm arising out of future such acts by him. The defendant may or may not have a conviction for a sexual (or any other) offence. The child or children to be protected must be under 16 (section 124(3)) or, for the purpose of the application of the section to Northern Ireland, 17 (section 124(8)).

253. *Subsection (1)* explains the circumstances in which a risk of sexual harm order may be made. The acts in *subsection (3)* which constitute the trigger behaviour for an order all involve explicitly sexual communication or conduct with or towards an child. The terms "image" and "sexual activity" are defined and an explanation is given in section 124(6) of when a communication is sexual. The types of behaviour at (3)(a) and (b) may amount to a criminal offence, for example under sections 10 to 13. However the trigger behaviour need not amount to criminal conduct. *Subsection (3)(c)* would cover a person giving condoms or a sex toy to a child. *Subsection (3)(d)* would cover a person sending pornographic images to a child over the Internet or describing the sexual acts he would like to carry out on the child. An order will not be made unless the court is satisfied (under *subsection (4)(b)*) that further such acts would cause a child or children physical or psychological harm (section 124(2)).

Section 124: Section 123: interpretation.

254. The definition of "image" at *subsection (4)* includes photographs, cartoon strips, email attachments and drawings. The use of the words "but regardless of any person's purpose" in *subsections (5)* to *(7)* means that an activity, or communication, or image, will only be "sexual" for the purposes of section 123 if a reasonable person, purely from the nature and circumstances of the activity, communication or image, would consider it to be sexual,

without having to enquire into the motive behind it. This catches activities or communications or images that, in all the circumstances, are explicitly or overtly sexual, for example a pornographic film or a description of oral sex. However, where for example a double entendre is used in communication, the reasonable person might have to consider the speaker's motive before he could decide whether the communication was sexual. So the use of the double entendre would not be "sexual" communication, for the purposes of section 123, as the term is defined in *subsection (6)*.

Section 125: RSHOs: variations, renewals and discharges

255. Section 125 provides for variations, renewals and discharges of risk of sexual harm orders. The procedure here is the same as that used to vary, renew or discharge a sexual offences prevention order imposed on an offender in the community (the application is by complaint to a magistrates' court), and is explained in the notes to section 108. (As the risk of sexual harm order is a new order, not a re-enactment, there is no equivalent provision to section 108(8)).

Section 126: Interim RSHOs

256. This section allows the police to apply for an interim risk of sexual harm order where an application has been made for a full order in respect of a defendant, but has not yet been determined. The interim order will be for a fixed period and will cease to have effect at the end of that period or, if earlier, when a decision is made on the full order.

Section 127: RSHOs and Interim RSHOs : appeals

257. The appeals process set out in this section is to be used where the defendant is challenging the imposition of an order. *Subsection (3)* provides that an order made by the Crown Court on an appeal against the granting of an order or interim order (other than an order in which the Crown Court orders that the application for an order or interim order be re-heard by a magistrates' court) is to be treated, for the purposes of determining where any application for variation, renewal or discharge of the order should be heard, as if it were made by the magistrates' court which made the original order (under sections 125(7) or 126(5)).

Section 128: Offence: breach of RSHO or Interim RSHO

258. It is a criminal offence to breach a risk of sexual harm order or interim risk of sexual harm order unless the defendant has a reasonable excuse for doing so.

Section 129: Effect of a conviction etc. of an offence under section 128

259. *Subsection (2)* relates to a defendant who is already a "relevant offender" (that is, subject to the notification requirements of this Part – see section 80) when convicted of an offence under section 128, or cautioned in respect of such an offence, or found not guilty of such an offence by reason of insanity, or found to be under a disability and to have done the act charged against him in respect of such an offence. Such a person will remain subject to the notification requirements for the duration of the "relevant order" (defined in *subsection (5)*). That is, he will remain subject to the notification requirements for the duration of the risk of sexual harm order that he breached, or if he breached an interim order, either for the duration of that order, or if a main order is made, the duration of the main order. However, if the notification period (see section 82) which originally applied to the person lasts for longer than the order, the person remains subject to the notification requirements until the end of that longer period.

260. *Subsection (3)* relates to those defendants who are not already subject to the notification requirements when convicted of an offence under section 128. Such a person will become subject to notification requirements as a result of that offence until the relevant order (explained above) ceases to have effect.

261. For the purpose of the notification requirements, the "relevant date" (see section 83) is the date when the person is convicted of the section 128 offence, or the date when he is cautioned in respect of it or when the relevant finding in respect of it is made. This means, for example, that the person must comply with the initial notification requirement (at section 83(1)) within 3 days of that conviction, caution, or finding.

Section 130: Power to amend Schedules 3 and 5

262. Section 130 allows the Secretary of State to amend by statutory instrument the list of offences in Schedules 3 and 5 and any of the age or sentence thresholds that apply to those offences. The offences listed in Schedule 3 trigger, providing the thresholds are met, the notification requirements of this Part of the Act. They can also be used, where the victim was under 16, to apply for a foreign travel order. The offences in Schedule 3 and Schedule 5 can trigger a sexual offences prevention order. Any amendment to Schedules 3 or 5, by adding an offence to them, will not extend the notification requirements of this Part retrospectively by, for example, making persons convicted of an offence added to Schedule 3 subject to the notification requirements, where they were convicted of that offence before the amendment was made. *Subsection (3)* provides, however, that it will be possible, where a new offence is added, for the police to apply for a sexual offences prevention order or an interim order or a foreign travel order in respect of an offender convicted or cautioned of that offence, or in respect of whom a relevant finding has been made relating to that offence, before the date of the amendment. The amending order will be subject to the affirmative resolution procedure (section 138(2)). For Scotland, the statutory instrument will be made by Scottish Ministers and laid before the Scottish Parliament.

Section 131: Young offenders: application

263. Young offenders are not sentenced to periods of imprisonment in the same way as adults. Section 131 therefore lists the sentences and periods of detention applicable to young offenders that should be considered as equivalent to a sentence of imprisonment for the purposes of working out the notification period and other purposes (e.g. section 81(3)(b)).

Section 132: Offences with thresholds

264. Section 132 provides that where an offence in Schedule 3 has a sentence (or other disposal, e.g. hospital order) threshold ("a sentencing condition"), the offender is to be regarded as having been convicted of that offence, or as having had a finding relating to that offence made in respect of him, only when the sentencing condition is met. This applies only to Part 2 of the Act. Establishing the date of a conviction or finding is important because it triggers the date when the notification requirements start to apply to the offender. For example, under section 83, an offender is required to make an initial notification at a police station within 3 days of the date of his conviction or finding for a relevant offence. In the case of offences with sentencing conditions, the notification requirements will only apply where the conditions are met and this will not be known until the offender is dealt with by the court. This could be some time after the conviction or finding in question. For example, a 25 year old who is convicted of sexual assault against a 20 year old woman would not be required to

'register' until he was sentenced to imprisonment for that offence or given an 12 month community sentence in respect of it by the court. *Subsection (3)* to *subsection (6)* cover foreign convictions and findings. These are relevant when determining whether to make a notification order and may be relevant in deciding whether to make a sexual offences prevention order or a foreign travel order. The effect of the subsections is the same as that of *subsection (3)* on convictions and findings in the United Kingdom, i.e. the date of the conviction or finding will be the date when the relevant sentencing conditions for the offence are met.

265. The offences in Schedule 5 (offences in relation to which which a sexual offences prevention order can be made) do not currently have sentencing conditions. However *subsection (4)* of section 130 provides a power which will enable the Secretary of State to amend sentencing conditions for offences in Schedules 3 and 5 in future. *Subsection (8)* of section 132 therefore extends the provisions to cover Schedule 5.

Section 133: Part 2: General interpretation

266. Section 133 defines certain terms used in this Part of the Act.

Section 134: Conditional discharges and probation orders

267. Section 134 provides that various provisions in other legislation to the effect that a conviction with absolute or conditional discharge is deemed not to be a conviction are not to apply for the purposes of this Part of the Act in relation to orders for conditional discharge made in respect of a post-commencement conviction.

Section 135: Interpretation: mentally disordered offenders

268. Section 135 clarifies how the provisions in this Part apply in respect of mentally disordered offenders.

Section 136: Part 2: Northern Ireland

269. This section makes a series of minor referential modifications necessary for the application and operation of Part 2 in Northern Ireland.

Part 3: General

Section 137: Service courts

270. Section 137 makes the modifications needed for provisions in Part 2 of the Act relating to court orders, convictions, findings, offences and proceedings to apply in the context of service courts (that is, courts-martial and Standing Civilian Courts) as well as in civilian courts. Service courts have jurisdiction to try all offences equivalent to an England and Wales criminal offence, including the most serious, committed outside the UK, and most such offences committed within the UK, by persons subject to Service law. These persons include Service personnel and, in limited circumstances, some groups of civilians, such as dependants or civil servants accompanying the Services overseas. Section 137 makes clear, for example, that if a person is convicted of a serious sexual offence by a court-martial, that person will be subject to the notification requirements. It also enables Service courts to impose sexual offences prevention orders at the time of sentencing in the same way as civilian courts. Where a Service court is satisfied that the test set out in section 104(1)(b) is met, namely that a sexual offences prevention order is necessary for the purposes of protecting the public in the UK from serious sexual harm, that court will be able to impose

such an order in the same way as a civilian court. However, section 137 provides Service courts with the power to impose a sexual offences prevention order only when dealing with an offender in respect of an offence listed in Schedule 3 or 5 and not following an application by the police.

Clause 141: Commencement

271. Clause 141 establishes a power for the Secretary of State to make a statutory instrument setting out how the measures included in this Act will come into force. *Subsection (2)* sets out what such an order may contain. It allows provision to be made for different parts of the Act to commence at different times. It also allows for the order to contain transitional provisions. Those provisions of the Act that are within the devolved competence of the Scottish Parliament will be commenced by the Scottish Ministers.

COMMENCEMENT

272. The provisions of the Act will come into force on such days that the Secretary of State or (where applicable) the Scottish Ministers specify by order under section 141.

HANSARD REFERENCES

Stage	Date	Hansard reference
Introduction (Lords)	28th January 2003	Vol. 643 Part No. 35 Col. 1012
Second Reading	13th February 2003	Vol. 644 Part No. 45 Col. 771-810 & 842-882
Committee day 1	31st March 2003	Vol. 646 Part No. 73 Col. 1048-1110 & 1127-1156
Committee day 2	1st April 2003	Vol. 646 Part No. 74 Col. 1170-1247 & 1255-1304
Committee day 3	10th April 2003	Vol. 647 Part No. 81 Col. 348-370 & 385-420
Committee day 4	28th April 2003	Vol. 647 Part No. 82 Col. 525-566
Committee day 5	13th May 2003	Vol. 648 Part No. 91 Col. 164–228
Committee day 6	19th May 2003	Vol. 648 Part No. 95 Col. 549 - 682
Report day 1	2nd June 2003	Vol. 648 Part No. 99 Col. 1049-1114 & 1131-1154
Report day 2	9th June 2003	Vol. 649 Part No. 104 Col. 11-25 & 47-116
Third Reading	17th June 2003	Vol. 649 Part No. 110 Col. 669-751

Introduction (Commons)	18th June 2003	
Second Reading	15th July 2003	Vol. 409 Part No. 129 Col. 177–252
Standing Committee B	9th September 2003	Col. 1–38
Standing Committee B	9th September 2003	Col. 39–92
Standing Committee B	11th September 2003	Col. 93–126
Standing Committee B	11th September 2003	Col. 127-168
Standing Committee B	16th September 2003	Col. 169–202
Standing Committee B	16th September 2003	Col. 203-246
Standing Committee B	18th September 2003	Col. 247–280
Standing Committee B	18th September 2003	Col. 281–314
Standing Committee B	14th October 2003	Col. 315–362
Standing Committee B	14th October 2003	Col. 363–410
Report and Third Reading	3rd November 2003	Vol. 412 Part no. 151 Col. 544-637
LCCA	13th November 2003	Vol. 654 Part No. 169 Col. 1605-1667
CCLM	18th November 2003	Vol. 413 Part No. 160 Col. 625-642
LCCM	18th November 2003	Vol. 654 Part No. 172 Col. 1911-1924
Royal Assent (Commons)	20th November 2003	Vol. 413 Col. 1037
Royal Assent (Lords)	20th November 2003	Vol. 654 Col. 2114

Printed in the UK by The Stationery Office Limited
under the authority and superintendence of Carol Tullo, Controller of
Her Majesty's Stationery Office and Queen's Printer of Acts of Parliament.